Business and Public Policy

Business and Public Policy

Edited by John T. Dunlop

DIVISION OF RESEARCH
GRADUATE SCHOOL OF
BUSINESS ADMINISTRATION
HARVARD UNIVERSITY
BOSTON • 1980

Distributed by Harvard University Press,
Cambridge, Mass. • *London, England*

Library of Congress Catalog Card No. 80-81866
ISBN 0-87584-119-8

Printed in the United States of America

Contents

1. Government Versus Business: An American
   Phenomenon   1
   Alfred D. Chandler, Jr.

2. The Abrasive Interface   12
   George P. Shultz

3. Business and the Public Policy Process   23
   Irving S. Shapiro

4. The Educational Opportunity   34
   John T. Dunlop

5. The Business-Government Problem: Inherent
   Difficulties and Emerging Solutions   39
   Richard G. Darman & Lawrence E. Lynn, Jr.

6. Educational Challenges in Teaching Business-
   Government Relations   65
   Hugo Uyterhoeven

7. Business and Public Policy   102
   John T. Dunlop

| Foreword

AS DEANS OF THE Graduate School of Business Administration and the School of Government, we believe the Program in Business and Government will be one of the most important ventures involving collaboration between members of our two faculties in the decade ahead. This program reflects Harvard's commitment to a strategy of collaboration among several of the university's graduate schools. The purpose of this joint effort is to fashion the university's most effective response to three urgent challenges.

The first challenge is government. The twentieth century has witnessed an unparalleled growth in the size and scope of government. During this century, federal government spending (in current dollars) has increased a thousandfold. Every working day, the U.S. government spends $2 billion —a sum greater than the annual expenditures of all but a small list of American corporations. State and local government spending has grown even more rapidly. Today, American governments—federal, state, and local—account for one-third of our gross national product. Moreover, budgetary comparisons understate the impact of government's growth. The *Federal Register,* which publishes government regulations, has swelled in the last thirty years from 2400 to over 60,000 pages.

Has this expansion in the size and role of government been informed by a coherent view of the strengths and weaknesses of government? Or, has government's growth resulted more from some combination of sharpened sensitivities and a political process in which problems, once identified, readily attract advocates of government as a solution?

Universities' first response must be to think harder about the role and size of government, the strengths and weaknesses of alternative forms of government action, and the impact of government's expansion on the balance between the public and private sectors. University-based research and reflection can contribute to the development of a clearer contemporary philosophy of government. Building on this nation's history, values, and Constitution, that philosophy must appreciate the genius of a mixed-enterprise society committed to individual rights, concerned for the common good, and driven by private action determined by private initiative. Government's role in setting the ground rules, refereeing the game, and intervening for special purposes must be recognized. But so also must the actions of private individuals, business firms, associations, and even universities in creating products and jobs, income and capital, knowledge, inspiration, and, ultimately, values.

A second challenge stems from the mounting evidence that the present adversary relationship between business and government does not serve society's interest. Current relations between the public and private sectors in the U.S. are marred by mutual ignorance, suspicion, and hostility. While this characterization applies across the board—indeed, not the least to relations between private universities and government—it is of greatest consequence in relations between business and government. The past decade has seen a vast expansion in the scope and detail of government intervention in what were once wholly private business decisions—interventions well beyond those of the New Deal, beyond traditional economic regulation, and beyond temporary wage and price controls. For most corporations, government is now a major determinant—often *the* major determinant—of the business environment. Too often, business and government find themselves in excessively polarized positions. The views of business that receive public attention often seem extreme and antisocial. To many business leaders, the actions of government appear not only ill-advised and ill-informed, but hostile in intent. Public policy suffers not simply from a lack of business confidence on issues of major national import, but from a lack of sophisticated and balanced contribution by *both* business and government in the process of policy development.

The challenge to which universities can respond is to help provide the knowledge and understanding from which a new working partnership between business and government can be constructed: one that encourages business, labor, consumers, and other parties to participate collaboratively in public policy making. University-based research, including especially well-documented cases of worst and best practice, can help leaders of all sectors learn that a posture of defensive reaction serves neither society's goals nor their own. The price of responsible citizenship is active participation in devising solutions to common problems. Recognizing that the specific interests of various parties compete, we must nonetheless recall that they compete within the framework of larger, shared objectives.

The third challenge stands at the main gate of the university: it is to equip general managers—both of the public and the private sectors—with the understanding and skills required for wise leadership in these new conditions. Here Harvard's strategy differs significantly from that of other institutions. This strategy recognizes that the growth of government and the increase in interactions between government and business pose special challenges for general managers, both in business and in government. But it does not minimize significant differences between public and private management. Harvard seeks, therefore, to build from the strength of its School of Business and its emerging School of Government a program that will promote interaction and mutual understanding between individuals training for private management and those training for public management —while preserving for each a proper discipline, integrity, and vitality.

Given the complexity of the problems and the far-reaching implications of government action, no sector in our society can rival government in its need for the ablest and best-trained minds. Yet the training provided public managers has traditionally been less adequate and more haphazard than that afforded businessmen, doctors, and lawyers. The mission of Harvard's School of Government is to provide serious, careful preparation for positions of public leadership. Following in the footsteps of the Business School, which was founded in the first quarter of this century, and the Law and Medical Schools in the preceding century, Harvard is committed to building a School of Government that serves society's demand for excellence in government in many of the ways Harvard's Schools of Business, Law, and Medicine meet that demand in their respective private professions. This entails a fundamental strategic choice: to build a professional school rather than a school of applied social science. By design, location (diagonally across the river from the Business School), and practice, the School of Government is committed to learning from the experience of Harvard's major professional schools. Thus, for example, as the School builds programs of teaching and research specifically tailored to the needs of government, the curriculum emphasizes case method instruction and the public management courses borrow transferrable aspects of private management.

Given their strategy, no relationship is more important to the School of Government than that with the Business School. Essential to the training of effective public managers is an understanding of business and an appreciation that in American society no major public purpose can be achieved by government acting alone. Effective government action can be essential to achieving major public purposes. Inept government action can prevent the realization of key public objectives. But whether the purpose be jobs or investments or adequate energy supplies or stable prices or new knowledge, success in achieving the public purpose requires an appropriate match between government action, on the one hand, and private action, on the other. Instruction in the School of Government must help public managers understand the ways government actions can create incentives, rather than disincentives, for private managers that encourage private actions that advance rather than retard public purposes.

The need in training general managers for business is, in many ways, the opposite side of the same coin. Without neglecting the knowledge and skills in finance, marketing, production and control that permit the chief executive officer to manage within the walls of his enterprise, the Business School curriculum recognizes that chief executives spend an ever increasing share of their time dealing with the environment outside the firm. The most important actor in this external environment is government. To be more than defensive or reactive to government, business leaders must learn to see problems from the perspective of public managers and to understand their incentives and constraints. Business practice is evolving rapidly in this regard. Effective training for business leadership must provide more understanding of the opportunities for business managers to be pro-active in helping solve public problems in ways that meet both public interests and those of their firm or industry.

The challenges are clear: government; relations between business and government; training for both public and private managers. Harvard's response is emerging. Building on the foundations laid over the last several decades, the Program in Business and Government makes more explicit and more focused the cooperative effort of our two Schools to develop faculty, curriculum, and training of the highest quality for general managers in business and for general managers in government.

As the papers in this volume argue persuasively, these challenges should engage the interests and the energy of the most thoughtful individuals in our society. As the Program in Business and Government takes shape, we look forward to working with the individuals who gathered for the inaugural seminar, and the many others who will profit from the papers printed in this volume, in this most promising venture.

Lawrence E. Fouraker, Dean 1970–1979
Graduate School of Business Administration
Graham T. Allison, Dean
School of Government

Introduction
Business and Public Policy

DEREK C. BOK

President, Harvard University

ONE OF THE GREAT transforming events in our
society over the last half-century has been the emergence of government as an active participant for
better or worse in all matters affecting the economy. This
transformation has helped the society to address a number
of important issues, but it also has created some very
troublesome problems.

We all recognize that the government will continue to
play a pervasive role in economic affairs, but none of us,
even including the representatives of government, can be
satisfied that we have as yet defined the appropriate role of
the state and private enterprise or that we have yet achieved
an effective working relationship between the two.

To resolve those problems will call for a great deal of
active cooperation from many people and from many institutions within our society. Among these institutions, universities have an important contribution to make. To put
the matter a bit more sharply, universities have not done
nearly enough over the past decades to address the problems

of effective business-government relations, and there is consequently a great deal that urgently needs to be accomplished to improve upon our record.

In the field of government, it is fair to say that universities have failed over a great many years to provide programs offering rigorous, professional preparation for important careers in the public sector that could compare in quality with the preparation traditionally given to the men and women entering the great private professions of law, business, and medicine.

In the field of business education, our knowledge, our competence, and our curricula have not been able to reflect adequately the fact that top executives everywhere today are having to devote a major share of their time and energy to a long list of extremely difficult problems resulting from regulatory, community, and legislative initiatives.

While acknowledging these deficiencies, Harvard, and other universities as well, have begun to make some major efforts over the last ten years to improve on past records. The School of Government has now been formed and has assembled an excellent faculty and a strong curriculum to prepare able people for important government positions.

The School has been wise enough to borrow from the Business School by concentrating not only on the teaching of recent college graduates but also on the development of executive programs for established public officials—newly elected congressmen, of whom we had over 40 just a few months ago, newly elected mayors, high-level defense officials and experienced civil servants.

At the Business School, under Dean Fouraker, many faculty members have likewise begun to pay serious attention to the role of government and its impact on business, and at least a score of the School's professors are engaged in teaching and research on business-government relations.

As those efforts go forward, there is not only an opportunity but a great need for active cooperation between the two Faculties. This is only a reflection of a larger need in the outside world, for in the future we will clearly have to have more businessmen who not only appreciate the shortcomings of government but also understand the way in which the government works, the political environment in which public policy is made, and the perspectives and imperatives that guide public officials and explain much of what they do. There is an equally pressing need for government officials who appreciate the problems of business, and who understand the difference between attractive policy blueprints or grand regulatory designs, and effective programs that will actually solve the problems at hand without placing intolerable burdens on private enterprise.

If we are to achieve this kind of understanding, this ability to appreciate the different points of view of these two sectors, that breadth of perspective will have to be fostered in the universities, and particularly in the professional schools that prepare young men and women for these two sectors of society. This is why we place such emphasis on fostering the closest possible relationship between our School of Business and School of Government.

To be specific about the kinds of cooperation that we have in mind and the kinds of cooperation we have already begun to introduce: we have encouraged collaborative research on such problems as improving the regulatory process and understanding better its effects on inflation, efficiency, innovation, and capital formation. Our principal goal has been to devise regulatory strategies to fit the problem at hand in ways that will solve it with the least possible burden and the fewest undesirable side effects. We have encouraged joint courses that will enable Business School students and students in the School of Government to work together and

learn together in studying issues of business-government relations. We have encouraged teaching by professors from
the School of Government within the Business School on
the legislative and the regulatory process. And we have
encouraged cooperation by Business School professors in
helping the Faculty of Government to understand how we
can adapt the methods and the principles of effective management to the very different environment of the public
sector and how we can expose students who will become
future government leaders to the practical problems of
public policy as they actually affect the business sector.

Because these issues are so enormous and important, we
have to make a substantial effort involving a broad agenda
of problems and a large number of faculty members. And
although much of that effort can emerge from able people
already at Harvard, we are actively developing the additional
human and material resources we need to make this enterprise successful.

But beyond the problem of resources, we also need to en-
list the active interest and participation of those who actually live the process of business-government relations
every day and experience at first hand its problems and
deficiencies.

The Business School already has a very long and successful tradition of working closely with its alumni and friends
to assist in developing courses and case materials and to
convey to the faculty a perceptive and realistic sense of the
current problems faced by businessmen. In fact, the entire
case method, which lies at the heart of the Business School,
has been made possible because of this cooperation between
businessmen and the professors at the School.

The School of Government, of course, is much newer, but
its master's program and its mid-career programs are already
producing an enthusiastic body of alumni who may be able

to play the same role in actively lending their advice and assistance to developing better programs to prepare people for important public sector positions. We hope that this program will help to launch a close and continuing collaboration between the faculties of the Business School and the School of Government and interested executives from public and corporate life.

Business and
Public Policy

1 | Government Versus Business: An American Phenomenon

ALFRED D. CHANDLER, JR.

Isidor Straus Professor of Business History
Harvard Business School

WHY IS IT THAT in the United States government and business have so often appeared as adversaries? Why has there not been more of the working relationships that characterize other advanced industrial nations? As one businessman, Crawford Greenwalt, the former chairman at DuPont, phrased the question: "Why is it that I and my American colleagues are being constantly taken to court—made to stand trial—for activities that our counterparts in Britain and other parts of Europe are knighted, given peerages or comparable honors?"[1] The

1. Greenwalt's statement was made to me when I had discussed with him background information for the chapter on DuPont in my *Strategy and Structure* (Cambridge, Mass., The MIT Press, 1962). For the Justice Department antitrust suit against I.C.I., see W. J. Reader, *Imperial Chemical Industries: A History*, Vol. II, Chs. 24 and 25, especially pp. 428–29.

This essay is based on information developed in the writing of *The Visible Hand: The Managerial Revolution in American Business* (Cambridge, Mass., 1977) and research I am currently doing or supervising on the rise of large-scale business enterprise in Europe and

Lords McGowan and Melchett, the senior executives of Imperial Chemical Industries, asked the same question about the American scene, when to their astonishment, the Attorney General of the United States hauled them into the New York District Court early in 1944 for violating the Sherman Antitrust Act, and at a time when they did almost no business in the United States. These questions asked often by businessmen and government officials are ones that intrigue the historian. Why, indeed, did not other countries develop antitrust and regulatory policies that helped to create an adversary relationship between government and business in the United States?

The question is particularly intriguing since such a relationship between government and business did not always exist in the United States. It came only with the sudden appearance of large-scale business enterprise in the last decade of the nineteenth century. Until the Civil War, business leaders remained involved in government at both local and national levels, and politicians were able businessmen. Textile manufacturers such as Nathan Appleton and iron makers such as Erastus Corning served as mayors and congressmen as well as local party leaders. The famed Albany Regency that ran the Democratic Party in New York state for years in the antebellum period included some of the state's most energetic business entrepreneurs.[2] As was true of Southern planters and Western farmers, businessmen of that day had the time and the interest to take an active part in government.

The separation between government and business came,

Japan. I am indebted to the Alfred P. Sloan Foundation, the German Marshall Fund, and the Division of Research for their support of this research.
2. As exemplified by the careers of C. C. Cambreleng, Azariah C. Flagg, and Samuel J. Tilden.

almost inevitably, as both business enterprise and government offices grew in size and complexity, in response to the opportunities and needs of a rapidly industrializing and urbanizing nation. With the coming of large-scale business enterprise, first on the railroads and then in industry, a new class of businessmen appeared—full-time salaried managers who made a lifetime career of working up the managerial ladder. Comparable administrative hierarchies came later in local and federal government. (They came first in the new cities to meet the needs for mass education and for a number of essential urban services.) At the federal level, the number of public administrators remained small until the coming of the Great Depression pushed the government into taking an active role in restoring the nation's economic health. Then with World War II and the continuing cold war, the number of government workers and administrators rose at an unprecedented rate. In no other country, however, were large managerial business hierarchies created before the formation of an extensive government civil service.

Numbers illustrate this point.[3] In the 1840s, there were only a handful of transportation and industrial enterprises that hired more than a single salaried manager. At the beginning of that decade, the total number of civilian employees (not just managers) in all government departments working in Washington totaled 1,014. By the 1890s when the railroads had already become giants and the industrials were not far behind, the federal establishment remained tiny. In 1890 when at least a dozen railroads employed over 100,000 workers, the civilian working force in Washington

3. U.S. Bureau of the Census, *Historical Statistics of the United States, Colonial Times to 1970* (Washington, D.C., 1975), pp. 1102–3, 1142; Chandler, *The Visible Hand*, pp. 204–5. For employment at General Motors and Standard Oil, see Chandler, *Strategy and Structure*, p. 50, and for the U.S. Steel Company, its *Annual Reports* for the 1920s.

numbered just over 20,000, and the nation's total military force—Army, Navy, and Marines—just under 40,000. By 1929, 68,000 civilians were employed by the government in Washington; and the total number of government employees came to just over 500,000, of which 300,000 were post office workers—the large majority of whom were being paid for political services rendered. In 1929, therefore, the government's working force in Washington was still a good deal smaller than that at United States Steel, General Motors, or Standard Oil (N.J.). Then the change began. By 1940 a million civilians worked for the federal government. By 1970, nearly three million did.

Because two sets of administrative hierarchies grew at different periods of time for different reasons to carry out different functions with different objectives, two quite different cultures appeared. The work, attitudes, and perspectives of the business manager and the civil servant became and remained almost as distinct and separate as those of the humanist and scientist—the two cultures C. P. Snow delineated many years ago. Nevertheless, the existence of two administrative cultures—one private and one public—can hardly account for the adversary relationship that grew up between them. The same two sets of administrators, the same two administrative cultures, appeared in Europe and Japan, but the relationship between them remained close. One underlying reason for this difference rests on the fact that in the United States the role, and with it the attitude, toward business of much of the federal government was defined before the creation of a professional class of public administrators.

In the United States, the coming of the large railroads and then of industrial enterprises with their extensive managerial hierarchies brought government regulation. The passage of the Interstate Commerce Act in 1887, the Sherman

Antitrust Act in 1890, and then the more precise Clayton and Federal Trade Commission Acts of 1914 provided the legislative framework for such regulation. In neither Europe nor Japan did any such comparable response occur. Why not?

One answer seems to be that in the United States the growth of big business appeared to threaten the well-being of other businessmen, but in Europe and Japan it did not. In the United States the railroad and the telegraph played a more central role in the nation's transportation and communication network than they did abroad, where existing roads, canals, and coastal shipping continued to carry a larger share of freight, passenger, and mail traffic. Moreover, by the 1880s American railroads, by far the largest business enterprises in the world, had come to be operated by professional managers whose primary objective was to keep their enterprises profitable. Managers set their rates according to costs and not to meet local or regional needs. Large shippers received lower rates then smaller ones, for the increased costs of carrying the larger shipment involved only those of adding a car or two. Similarly, the cost of carrying freight from one major commercial center to another was often less than carrying it to many points not directly on the through route. Such discriminations between shipper and place, understandable in terms of railroad economics, often determined the success or failure, even the economic life or death, of business enterprises and whole communities. The threatened smaller shippers and the less favored communities protested vigorously, and they had the numbers to assure them the political power necessary to bring Congress to pass a law creating a regulatory commission to determine just and reasonable rates. As Lee Benson and other scholars have pointed out, it was not the farmers but the merchants and shippers who pressed for railroad regulation.[4] With the passage of the Hepburn Act of 1906, which gave the commission real power, major rate changes were decided in the courts by adversary procedures between the railroads and the commission.

Much the same type of businessmen—the older general merchants and the newer specialized wholesalers—provided similar pressures that led to the enforcement of the Sherman Act in the early years of the 20th century and the passage of the Clayton and Federal Trade Commission Acts in 1914. Even more than small manufacturers, these middlemen felt themselves threatened by the rise of large-scale industrial enterprise in the 1880s and 1890s. This was because manufacturing firms grew large by integrating forward in marketing, backwards into purchasing, and by obtaining their own raw materials. In so doing, they replaced the wholesaler with their own salesmen and buyers who sold directly to the retailers and bought directly from farmers, processors, and producers. Such new giants as American Cotton Seed Oil, National Linseed Oil, Distillers-Securities, American Sugar Refining, American Tobacco, Quaker Oats, Corn Products, such flour makers as Pillsbury and Washburn, canners such as Borden, Heinz and Campbell soup, meat packers such as Armour and Swift, brewers such as Anheuser-Busch and Pabst, all sold consumer goods in the national and international markets and purchased their materials from agricultural exchanges or the farmers themselves. Others such as Standard Oil in kerosene, and Procter & Gamble and Colgate in soap, Sherwin-Williams in paint, Parke-Davis in drugs, also sold branded consumer goods in the national and world markets. In every case, these new managerial hierarchies replaced the wholesalers with their own salaried em-

4. Lee Benson, *Merchants, Farmers and Railroads* (Cambridge, Mass., Harvard University Press, 1955).

ployees and managers. At the same time, these same middle-men were reeling from the impact of the new giant retailers —the department stores, the mail-order houses such as Sears and Montgomery Ward, and the new chain stores like A&P and Woolworth's. Under this onslaught the proportion of goods distributed by wholesalers, the most influential businessmen in hundreds of small American towns and cities, was cut in half between 1889 and 1929.[5]

So powerful was the resulting protest that the regulation of business became the paramount domestic issue in American politics in the early twentieth century. In 1912—one of these rare national elections in which there were four rather than two major candidates—all four promised in somewhat different ways to regulate and control business. Moreover, by business all four meant big business operated through managerial hierarchies and not small personal enterprise. The hostility toward large firms lessened during the prosperous years of the twenties but returned in full force in the thirties when big business took the blame for the economic woes of the Depression. Then in the sixties and seventies, business, particularly big business, was quickly blamed for the depletion of resources and the pollution that resulted, almost inevitably, from the unprecedented output of our huge industrial economy. By then, the standard American response to complex economic problems was to pass laws creating regulatory commissions to monitor the activities of the businesses involved.

Why did this not happen elsewhere? Why didn't other nations adopt similar laws and create comparable regulating commissions? One reason, as previously suggested, was that the rise of large-scale enterprise in Europe and Japan had

5. Harold Barger, *Distribution's Place in the American Economy Since 1869* (Princeton, Princeton University Press, 1955) pp. 69–71.

much less of an adverse affect on the fortunes of other business groups. In Western Europe the railroads were fitted into an already efficient network of roads, canals, rivers, and coastal shipping. There, as distances were much smaller and communities already established, economies of railroad rate making brought less discrimination between persons and places. On the continent the railroads were built and operated by existing public administrative hierarchies. The railroad system in France, for example, became and remains still the creation and creature of the Corps des Pontes et Chasseurs. Civil servants operating these noncompetitive enterprises were under much less pressure to base rates on costs and to discriminate between shippers and communities in order to maintain profits or to get business from competitors, and they were under more pressure to meet the needs of shippers and communities in the regions in which they served. In Britain where the railroads were built and operated privately, the merchants and industrialists who promoted them kept a closer control over their affairs than did those in the United States. As early as the 1850s they had worked out schemes for pooling traffic that eliminated the competitive pressures and discriminations that plagued American railroads until the Interstate Commerce Commission took over rate making and rate enforcing.

Of more importance, the new giant industrial firms did not replace existing wholesalers. In Germany and France very few large firms appeared in the consumer goods industries. There were very few giant food, tobacco, vegetable oil, flour, sugar, soap, paint, or drug companies until well after World War II, and those few sold largely in bulk to wholesalers. The large enterprises came instead in the producers' goods industries—in metals, chemicals, machinery, and other industries whose products were not distributed through the wholesalers' network. In Britain, the first industrial nation and therefore the first to import food and other materials on a massive scale, large consumer goods enterprises did appear. However, because the domestic market was geographically small (nearly every part of the United Kingdom could be reached in a day); because there existed a well-established marketing and distribution network before the coming of the railroad; and because the existing industrial families disliked weakening the control of their enterprises by hiring managers—for these three reasons, the new large food, drink, soap, and drug firms continued to rely on the existing wholesalers and other middlemen to distribute their products and to obtain their new materials. Only in the twenties and thirties did they begin to build buying and marketing organizations similar to those created by American firms forty or fifty years earlier. As these industrialists relied heavily on overseas markets and supplies, they did set up branch sales and buying offices particularly in the Commonwealth nations. That expansion abroad, however, did not affect the middleman at home. As a result, even though there was a strong antimonopoly strain in the economic thought of the British middle class, no group felt the urgency to put pressure on the government to provide instruments to control and regulate concentrated economic power. In Britain, protests resulting from industrial changes also dominated domestic politics in the early twentieth century; but the protest came, not from the middle class, but from the workingmen, who unlike their American counterparts, formed political parties to battle for higher wages and better conditions of work and life.

If the growth of the large-scale enterprise in consumer goods did not create pressures, as it did in the United States, for government to regulate business, its growth in producers' goods positively encouraged a closer relationship between the two. In Europe and Japan, where public hierarchies had been established long before private ones, makers of chemicals, metals, and machinery were far more dependent on foreign markets than were American producers. Industrialists in those countries quickly looked to public officials to help them win and hold overseas trade. The civil servants were willing to oblige by permitting cooperation and cartelization at home and by using diplomacy and even force abroad to keep open markets and sources of supply. They did so because they believed that economic strength abroad enhanced the nation's position in international diplomacy and politics. Cartels at home did indeed help the German and French to expand abroad. Even in laissez-faire Britain, the Board of Trade encouraged, before World War I, government participation in what would become British Petroleum. During the war the government sponsored the British Dyestuff Corporation. Then in 1926 it encouraged the giant merger that became Imperial Chemicals Industries. The creation of that near monopoly was the achievement that helped to bring both Sir Harry McGowan and Sir Alfred Mond [Lord Melchett] their peerages. As Crawford Greenwalt complained, a comparable merger in the United States would have instantly brought an antitrust case. Indeed, as soon as the success of American arms began to encourage the exporting of the American way of life, the Justice Department did bring the lords McGowan and Melchett and their Imperial company into court.

Here, then, is an historian's answer to the question Mr. Greenwalt used to ask. In the United States, business hierarchies appeared before public ones. In Europe, the reverse was true. When the large government bureaucracies did come in this country, the basic role of government toward business had already been defined; and that definition developed largely as a response of an influential segment of the business community to the rise of modern big business. A comparable response did not occur abroad. There, on the one hand, big business did not appear as such a sharp and sudden threat to small business as it did in the United States. On the other hand, both public and private administrators saw mutual advantages in cooperating to expand overseas trade.

The adversary relationship developed in the United States had its benefits. Cooperation and cartelization, for example, did hold back technological innovation. As an ICI executive visiting Wilmington in 1937 observed: "The most striking difference between DuPont's business and ours arises from the existence of free competition in America."[6] By that he meant that DuPont's research was not held back by cartel-like agreements, not only those with other companies, but even with other divisions within the company. But such an adversary relationship also certainly had its costs as both George Shultz and Irving Shapiro will make very clear in the two following chapters.

Lessons can be learned from history. The lesson of the story just told is not that the past determines the future, but rather that a study of the past can suggest ways to redefine the relationship between business and government administrators so that the nation can receive benefits without paying unnecessary costs. By embarking on a public policy program, the Harvard schools of government and business are taking a major step toward that redefinition.

6. Reader, *Imperial Chemical Industries*, II, 93.

2 | The Abrasive Interface

GEORGE P. SHULTZ

President, Bechtel Corporation

COMMON TALK THESE DAYS around the board and conference tables of business is about the overbearing omnipresence of government in every aspect of business operations. Government is no longer just Robin Hood, but some combination of Louella Parsons and Edward G. Robinson. The businessman, trying to conduct his operations in a reasonably efficient way, is increasingly joining Jimmy Durante in the lament "everybody wants to get into the act."

Speaking as a businessman of about five years now, I can vouch for the fact that there is plenty to complain about. Government seems to be your opponent, not your friend, or even a neutral referee. Nevertheless, during my years in government, the situation looked a little different. These contrasts in my business and government experience embolden me to set out here suggestions about *how* each party might better approach the abrasive business-government interface and *what* areas might better be eliminated from it.

While in the government, I found a great variety among

those who visited me from business. An important dimension of variability involved the homework done by the visiting businessman. Many came in very poorly prepared, with only general complaints and groans and without real substance to back up their points or practical suggestions for dealing with them. Many of these petitioners probably went away feeling that I was unresponsive and unsympathetic. Increasingly, however, it seemed to me that businessmen were learning that homework pays off. This is not simply a matter of being factually informed and reasonably objective in presentation. It also means looking beyond the very narrow interests of the individual firm or industry and offering some connection between what you want and broader public interest. Sometimes this contrast between the poorly informed, narrow interest and the well-informed connection to a broader interest is emphasized by reliance of the former on an often naked reference to political clout. As one who spent about a decade in Mayor Daley's Chicago, I know that clout can be for real. On the other hand, I can think of many sights I would rather see unadorned and which would not produce the same combination of skepticism and resentment.

Examples of effective business efforts are increasingly easy to come by and would be well worth studying in the dispassionate setting of the university. Take the difficult issues posed by legislation dealing with the Arab boycott of Israel. Their complexities—rationalizing conflicting national laws into rules of conduct for international commerce—are immense, the stakes are high, and the associated passions intense. With skillful and creative leadership from Irving Shapiro, the Business Roundtable tackled these issues in a sophisticated and professional manner. Through discussions with leading representatives of various Jewish groups, a legal task force was set up through which negotiations on the issues took place. Congressional and executive branch groups were kept apprised of these negotiations, and the agreement reached in these private negotiations was accepted by them (most likely with considerable relief) and embodied literally into the law on a word-for-word basis. Here the business people involved did have high stakes of their own on the table, but they went at the task cognizant of the broader interests involved and with the help of thoroughly professional people.

Another type of effective business action is illustrated by a recently issued study undertaken by the Business Roundtable of the costs of government regulation. Here, again, business people conducted a careful and professionally managed research effort. The results show that certain categories of costs can be identified and measured and that they are substantial and growing. The study also takes due notice of the additional large, though unmeasurable, costs of regulatory uncertainty—a real wild card in investment decisions. This study has been made widely available in Washington and most probably will contribute not only to constructive discussion of this hot topic but also to the impact of statements made by business leaders about regulatory overkill. Let us hope so. The pace of capital formation and productivity is at stake. Attention from top businessmen, speaking with credibility, must be joined to important, substantive proposals in an effective combination.

Still another example very much in the formative stage right now is the debate over and ratification of the agreements concluding the Tokyo Round of trade negotiations. There is no subject as domestic as international trade. Nowhere is the conflict between the general benefits derived from more open trade and the difficulties for certain special interests more starkly portrayed as in this field. These are important agreements, and the business reaction to them will make a real difference in their acceptability to Congress.

Businessmen will be on the spot to do their homework and to pursue their interests in an enlightened manner. The temptation will always be there to move from making a speech about the evils of governmental intervention in business affairs to arguing in a congressional office for governmental protection of a special and vulnerable interest..

Moving to a different area, take the problem of blame and responsibility, as illustrated by the question of inflation, what causes it and how it can be cured. Inflation, including our current roaring version, is rooted in government policy and behavior. However broad the agreement in the truth of this observation, even in occasional presidential statements, the practical outcome seems to be—almost as though drawn toward it by a magnet—some form of wage and price controls. In fact, today's version of controls seems like a rerun of an old movie. I didn't like them in the early seventies and I don't like them any better now. This is one old movie we should keep in the can. As these controls move into center stage, unwillingness to conform with them becomes conveniently tagged as the reason for inflation, and those unwilling to conform the villains. Maybe such scapegoating is good politics, but it is certainly lousy economics, and it contributes to the abrasive interface in a predictable manner.

We can all recall times when a president or his spokesman has lashed out at "inflationary" price increases in some major industry. Lately, to the discomfort of purists, some major businesses have been taking the view that they are not going to be put into a no-win political corner. On the contrary, they have said to the President, "we will help you beat on everybody in sight, including labor." In the process, labor emerges as the bad guy, ironically, for upholding the principles of freedom of institutions and markets and the sanctity of private contracts—along with its own interests. More abrasion, but with an added dimension.

At any rate, scapegoating by government at the expense of business and labor has certainly helped to poison the atmosphere. Lines of worthwhile inquiry here go beyond the *substance* of blame/responsibility type issues—Why inflation? Why energy problems?—into *processes* that may help reduce the abrasive outcome, for example, how to hold private discussions between government and labor-management representatives.

Who Should Do What?

Basic differences in the structure of authority in business and government add to the potential abrasiveness of the interface. And reflection on these differences raises questions about the comparative advantage of business and government for various important tasks. I think of government as having a deliberately flat organizational structure, stemming from the very concept of checks and balances. The resulting disposition to delay has been compounded in recent years with action-stopping power more widely distributed in Congress and the executive branch. Government action is crab-like at best, with an overwhelming emphasis on policy formation as opposed to execution. Though, as Will Rogers put it, we may "be thankful we're not getting all the government we're paying for," it would be nice for the government to get out of the way occasionally.

By contrast, the pyramidal structure of organization found in most textbooks does reasonably resemble the reality of business. A "doing" organization must be set up to force the decisiveness that gets action. One of the first lessons learned in moving from government to business is that, in business you must be careful when you tell someone who is working for you to do something, because the probability is high that he will do it. In government, no way; among other things, he doesn't necessarily consider himself to be really working for you in the first place. Perhaps these variations in the structure of authority can be appropriately thought of in terms of rather different incentive systems in these two worlds. In government and politics, recognition and therefore incentives go to those who formulate policy and maneuver legislative compromise. By sharp contrast, the kudos and incentives in business are with the person who can get something done. It is execution that counts. Who can get the plant built, who can bring home the sales contract, who can carry out the financing, and so on.

This contrast between "debating" and "criticizing" organizations with their disposition to delay and "doing" organizations with their spirit of action adds to the abrasiveness of the government-business interface. The well-publicized events surrounding Sohio's effort to move oil from the West coast inland by pipeline show how frustrating, let alone costly, the processes of debate and criticism can be, and they also show that business may be led simply to throw up its hands and walk away.

Sohio began in January 1975 the process of securing necessary permits and governmental approvals: a total of approximately 700 permits were required from about 140 local, state, federal, or private agencies. On March 13, 1979, fifty months later, the decision was reached to abandon the project. In the interim, Sohio had spent $50 million and managed to secure only 250 of the 700 permits. When they abandoned the project, they were spending at a rate of $1 million per month in the approval procedures. What's left is government regulating a pipeline that doesn't exist.

The volume of permits and governmental bodies before whom Sohio had to appear suggests another aspect of the problem. Adam Smith once remarked that specialization increases with the size of the market. Well, perversely, the vast increase in regulation in recent years has been accomplished by a form of specialization that amounts to a balkanization of problems. A whole host of federal, state, and local agencies regulate various aspects of what to a business is one problem. The legitimate concern is not just a matter of the time involved to go to so many different places for answers. Action can be completely hung up by differences of view among those who represent regulatory interests that are deliberately insulated from each other by statute. A friend once remarked that whatever is not prohibited nowadays is required. I am forced to amend his statement to—whatever is prohibited may also be required.

All this leads to a central tension that exists in our system of political economy, pulling and hauling at the institutions of business and government—a tension between the essential goals of economic efficiency and political equity. If better understood and handled, this tension can be a creative force and can help us thread our way to a better division of labor between business and government.

Within the private sector, competition forces efficiency on businessmen and financiers, whether they like it or not. Indeed, one can say that those in public or private life who have resources placed in their hands must—almost as a matter of trust on behalf of society—see that those resources are used as productively as possible. So the business and financial system marches to the drummer of efficiency.

But not so the political system. Most politicians will nod to efficiency, but it is usually little more than a nod. The drummer that the politician marches to is equity. When a problem comes up, economic thinking says, "What is the efficient way to solve it?" Political thinking says, "What is the equitable solution?" In any exercise in political economy, these two distinct patterns of thought are interacting, and the task at hand is to see how they can be meshed where they *must be,* but sought separately where they *can be.*

Renewed emphasis on the idea of competence can help with this task. We need to recognize that a given organization or aggregation of people cannot do everything. Competence is important and it demands specialization. The more any organization attempts, the more the limits of its competence will become apparent. The widely advertised "crisis of confidence" may more truly be a crisis of competence.

In business, the bottom line is pretty obvious. Business graveyards are full of companies that tried to do things they didn't know how to do and were shot down by the competitive system. The point is as true of governments, but the bottom line, no less present, is more elusive. As politicization of more and more of our economic and private life has extended the reach of government, it has led government officialdom more and more into areas with which they are fundamentally unfamiliar. Exhibitions of incompetence bring a general lack of confidence—one of the driving forces behind last year's widespread tax revolt, an instance of government's bottom line.

The field of energy today illustrates in spades the problems raised for efficiency by the use of price controls imposed in the name of equity, as well as the results of an inappropriate division of labor between regulation and the marketplace.

The difference between what our government said about energy and what it has done is truly amazing. Unfortunately for our country, this is not just a minor inconsistency, but is an exercise in energy doublespeak with potential consequences of vast proportions both at home and abroad.

We have suppressed the price of domestically produced

oil and gas, and in one master stroke our government has produced these results:

- A subsidy for imported oil, thereby encouraging its use and generating a level of demand that helps sustain world oil prices.
- A reduction in the incentives to find and produce more oil and gas in the United States.
- An incentive to consumption of these and other forms of energy by keeping the price below what is paid in most other consuming countries.

Beyond these direct effects, the suppression of the price makes necessary the allocation of supplies by an exceedingly complex set of regulations administered by a large and growing bureaucracy. These regulations and arbitrary changes in them face any investor with substantial political risks, which in turn simply raise the rate of return necessary to justify a new venture. And, as a result of government double-speak on energy, in the five years that have elapsed since the October 1973 Arab oil embargo, our dependence on foreign oil has increased dramatically.

We have supplies of coal within the United States, we keep telling ourselves, that can last us for centuries. All we have to do, we keep telling ourselves, is mine it and burn it, thereby converting coal into that most versatile and essential underpinning of our economy, electrical energy. Here again, however, regulations abound at all stages of this process, and they become more severe with each legislative session and issue of the Federal Register. For example, the EPA has proposed new air pollution rules which would preclude the use of virtually all of the high-sulfur midwestern coal, even after coal washing and flue gas scrubbing. In the process, mining becomes an ever more risky business, and burning coal becomes literally impossible in certain (not necessarily heavily populated) parts of the country. Once again doublespeak: bursts of rhetoric encouraging the use of coal accompanied by regulations that make it unnecessarily expensive and sometimes prohibitively so.

Why not let the system of markets and enterprise go to work on the energy problem in the name of an efficient solution to a problem of central importance to our country? We can find better ways to serve the goal of equity than piggybacking on the rhetoric of poverty and failing to price ourselves into development of our indigenous sources of energy.

Coping with the abrasive interface comes down to using a few simple ideas:

- Return to the concept of limited purpose organizations, where government as well as business, universities, and other organizations undertake the responsibilities of their comparative advantage and tread lightly, if at all, elsewhere.
- Recognize that running major industries or enterprises, either directly or indirectly through detailed regulation dictating how to get the work done, is not the government's bag.
- Recognize as businessmen that attention to homework is really a necessary condition to consideration of your point of view by government and, for that matter, the general body politic.
- Stay away—both government and business—from recourse to scapegoating, which leads people to lose sight of the merits of issues, subverting reality to political posturing.

A final note: The community looks to the universities for the ideas, the objectivity, and the analysis that will help us think through such problems as how to handle the abrasive government-business interface. Business and government both have, themselves, developed greater capacity for research and understanding than in earlier days. If they bring more to the party, they need more than ever the perspective of genuine scholarship. The interaction in universities, here and in a few other places, of centers for business and government study, augurs well for the effort needed.

3 | Business and the Public Policy Process

IRVING S. SHAPIRO

Chairman, E. I. du Pont de Nemours & Company

THE DUAL TEST of an organization is how well it performs its chosen functions and how well it matches the values of the society which charters it. If it is competent but hostile to the mores of the community, or acceptable in that regard but incompetent in its delivery of goods or services, then it forfeits its legitimacy.

Business and government, two of the giants of contemporary society, have not been winning very high marks on this test in recent years. Each has tried to improve its standing with the public, with no great success.

The focal points of public discontent are familiar. Government is seen as overgrown and inefficient, given to the protection of its own bureaucratic legions, corrupted by special interest groups, and unresponsive to the needs of the ordinary citizens who are forced to pay for good government without getting it.

Business, particularly big business, is seen as an uncontrolled power that bends the political process to its will and is not sincerely concerned with the quality of its products or the safety and security of the people whose lives it affects —which is to say, just about everybody.

It is not my purpose to go into any detail on the sad decline of institutional reputations. I would, however, like to push beyond these to some observations about business leaders and public policy makers, specifically to make the point that leaders in both camps must understand their missions differently and act differently in the future if the American society is to be served.

In the fall of 1978, John Dunlop presented a paper making a three-part point:

He said first that there has been a fundamental change in the political process, due to the "massive new penetration [by government] into all manner of heretofore private economic activity."

Second, that neither the leaders of business nor those of government have adapted to this state of affairs by learning to live and work with each other.

And third, that their failure to do so has potentially disastrous consequences.[1]

I agree and want to expand on that. What is needed is not just a little better perspective all around, or a little more communications. What is needed is a basic change in the way leaders define their jobs and operate in the public policy area.

What is needed is an understanding in both business and government that these institutions are merely means to an end in our society. Neither is ordained by Holy Writ. Both have to show that they are doing what society wishes, not just what they themselves might wish.

What is needed are some new premises about the right and proper relationship between business and government.

1. John T. Dunlop, "Growth, Unemployment and Inflation," in *Economic Growth,* Sub theme 1, 26th Congress, International Chamber of Commerce, Paris, France, 1978.

For a long time the two have been circling around each other like gladiators in combat, blocking and parrying each other's moves. That may amuse some of the spectators, but too often it results in poor government policies and lousy business decisions. You get programs grounded in vindictiveness rather than practicality, and all the while enormous amounts of energy are being put into adversarial politicking that could more properly be used to resolve the nation's real problems.

It's healthy to keep business and government at arm's length, with everyone behaving in a way he would not mind being reported in the newspapers, assuming all the facts could be exposed. However, an arm's length relationship doesn't require the kind of hostility that we have seen in recent years.

What the nation needs from business and government is an understanding that neither one of those institutions has a monopoly on intelligence or probity, or the wisdom to prescribe all by itself for the public welfare. Such understanding can be built only through education and experience.

There is a lot more involved here than simply being competent at your craft. People heading for careers in government and those turning toward business need exposure to each other's theology. There is a need for people in government to understand the dynamics of economic processes and to have some feeling for the workings of the business organizations that fulfill so many of our nation's economic functions. That logic can be flipped over to apply to business people understanding government.

This is not intended as a lecture on the educational structures that are most appropriate to this task. (Harvard has been in education even longer than Du Pont has been in business, so I defer to seniority.) All I want to say is that this new approach is appealing because it recognizes that it is artificial to think of business education as separate from education in government.

The outside world no longer tolerates such a split.

I gave you Professor Dunlop's three-part proposition. Shapiro's has only two:

First, the role of the business executive in America, and certainly the role of the chief executive officer of any sizable enterprise, has changed to such a degree that we are now bringing forward a new breed of manager.

Second, business executives are learning to live with their "common law" partner, the government. They are taking a few bruises in the bargain, but that's a small price to pay for an on-the-job education in how the system works and how to figure out what is practical and what isn't. The central fact is that executives have come to see that this is something they have to learn to run their businesses properly, and to make the American system work better—that being as much a duty for a business executive as anyone else.

There is a lot of rhetoric about the "tides of change" in our country, but that simile does not apply here. Tides come in and go out again. The tide discussed here came in, and it is staying.

The only practical course is to regard as essentially permanent the system that has evolved. Call it what you will, "quasi-public," "half-free enterprise," "the mixed economy" —by any name, it is a system in which heavy governmental involvement will remain a fact of life for business. A company such as Du Pont can expect government to continue to tell us whether or not we can build a plant at a chosen location. GM and Ford can expect the government to continue to help them design cars. All of us can expect government to continue to tell us what fuel to burn in the furnace, what sort of affirmative action we should take in hiring and promotion, and how many pounds, if not tons, of reports we shall submit.

Without suggesting for a minute that the private sector ought to take all this lying down, it has to be admitted that some of the government's involvement is desirable, and another piece of it is probably inevitable at least for the short term. The job is to live with that situation even as we try to improve it, and the basic lesson to learn is that government and business operate in different environments. What makes a convincing case in one of them may seem almost irrelevant in the other.

As the Washington columnist David Broder has said, government is a process of struggle and accommodation, not an exercise in applied theology. On a given day politics may outweigh economic and technological facts; at another time, or with the issue handled differently, the facts might carry the day. It follows that forecasts based on economic efficiency alone, or scientific probabilities, have limited predictive power in government. A businessman trained in the classical way finds this baffling, not to say illogical.

There has been a pronounced trait in government toward "one issue thinking," that is, toward focusing on singular problems without much concern for related ones. This is a luxury that most leaders in society simply cannot afford. Derek Bok as president of Harvard has to think about multiple constituencies: faculty, students, alumni, the neighbors in Cambridge and Boston, and the fund givers in the foundations and the grant givers in Washington, not to mention the regulatory agencies. People in jobs like mine have similar sets of constituencies and overlapping concerns and have to try to balance them all.

It would be nice to report that people in political life are also bound to think about problems in the round. They may be so inclined, but the plain fact is that in practice they often go with a "single issue" decision. Maybe it's because they think that otherwise they may be licked at the polls. Maybe the law as it's written gives them no other choice. Maybe they are listening to pressure groups that are deliberately trying to narrow the issues on the grounds that a wider debate will only weaken their case.

Whatever the reason, it's a mistake to suppose that an overall balanced view is going to surface on its own within the government. It is most surely a mistake to suppose that your own point of view, based on whatever supporting evidence you have, is going to be given due emphasis—or even noticed at all—unless your team makes an effort to sell it.

Maybe that will happen, and maybe not. An example on the negative side was offered by Senator Hubert Humphrey shortly before his death. Reminiscing about the days when the Congress was considering the creation of the Occupational Safety and Health Administration, Senator Humphrey said that the key decisions were made without much talk about what it all would cost. It seems that not much more attention was given, either, to the possibility that equal or better results on safety might have been gained in other ways than through another new federal agency. OSHA had been proposed, and OSHA is what we got. (In fairness to Senator Humphrey, he was commenting on this with regret, not pride.)

Leaders in business are learning to look realistically at the governmental climate and to learn from their own past mistakes. They are becoming personally involved, not standing on the sidelines saying, "I couldn't make any difference, anyway," and relying exclusively on their paid lobbyists and trade associations.

Executives are realizing that the day is gone when the spot at the top of an organization chart permitted a private lifestyle. A generation or two in the past, you could get by in business by following four rules: stick to business, stay out of trouble, join the right clubs, and don't talk to reporters. Some of us may yearn for that bygone era, but we have to take life as it comes, and today's executive is more often in the midst of the fray. CEO's are now to be found tramping through the corridors in Washington and the state capitals, testifying, talking with elected representatives and administrative aides, pleading cases in the agency offices and occasionally in the White House. Reporters are learning our names and finding that many more of us have our doors open.

Business leaders are beginning to understand the territory. They have learned, for instance, that to understand tax policy you have to understand Russell Long as well as what is written in the tax code. Businessmen have learned that there often is a difference between what is said politically and what is meant—which tells you there may be room for compromise behind the rhetoric.

Executives are learning to leave their personal politics at home and work with people in government on both sides of the aisle, not sacrificing their basic principles, but looking at issues on the merits alone and not along party lines. Businessmen gain nothing in government by making "enemies" lists, or by talking only to congressmen of comfortable ideology. Washington leaders who may oppose business on one issue may on another issue join in a coalition in business' favor.

For example, the vote in Congress that killed the bill that would have set up a new independent consumer protection agency was not made just by the certified friends of business. That bill went under because people with a lot of different political leanings came to the conclusion that this wasn't the way to solve the problem. If several dozen existing agencies weren't doing whatever protecting the consumer needs, Congress decided that the right course of action was to make those agencies function better, not to add another layer of bureaucracy.

A case in which I have personal involvement is Senator Metzenbaum's effort to change the patterns of corporate governance. I am totally at odds with the senator's proposals, yet I have sat with his advisory committee and tried to be an effective minority voice. I probably didn't convert anybody, but my theory is that you have zero chance of scoring points unless you get into the game, and it is just possible that you might learn something from other points of view.

One other bit of territorial savvy is that, by its structure, government places a great deal of power in the hands of some people who are relatively little known, who have little experience, and who may not be in the same job or committee slot very long. To ignore such individuals, to try to deal instead only with the stars of first magnitude, is a great mistake: Those lesser lights are probably intelligent, energetic —and the true authors of the bill some senator will present to his peers tomorrow morning.

What are the central observations here? Out of all the hits and misses and new-found points of contact, what basically does a chief executive need to know about government to do his job and make the system work better? It seems that the business leaders most successful in working with government, those who best represent the new breed, share several traits.

First, they arm themselves with facts. They put significant corporate resources into this effort, plus a big chunk of their own time. When the job has been done very well and the documentation has been made nearly bulletproof, an interesting thing has happened: people in government have displayed a new attitude toward the businessmen. The government people have concluded that these folks might just know what they are talking about and can be trusted.

That sword has two edges, of course. If a business executive abuses that trust, if the facts don't hold up and the government people are left out on a limb, that executive will be long into retirement before he is trusted again.

Simply having the facts, even presenting them in person and effectively, is no guarantee of an acceptable outcome, but it works a remarkable number of times; and the alternative—not having the facts—is usually fatal.

A second trait the leaders in the forefront have in common is their willingness to try new approaches. When the Arab nations announced their boycott of companies doing business with Israel, it was people in business as well as government, together with leaders of interested Jewish organizations, who were able to arrive at a compromise policy recommendation, and it was from this support base that the House and Senate enacted a law to deal with this problem. It is not a perfect solution by any means, but it is far better than the alternative moves that would otherwise have been taken.

One encouraging note from that example is that people in government showed that they, too, were willing to look for a new approach.

A third component is the recognition that to work effectively with government, business must come up with positive alternatives, not just negatives. In view of the decades of opposition by some business representatives to almost every step government decided to take—decades in which the final score was like Charlie Brown's baseball team: fifty for them, zero for us—it ought to be clear that knee-jerk opposition is at best a delaying tactic.

The objective is not to win delays but to improve the outcome, and to that end business leaders must come for-

ward with positives. By the time a Congressional committee
is laboring over a bill, it has long since been decided that:
(1) there is a problem, and (2) government ought to be
doing something about it. The decision may be in error on
both counts, but it is an uphill battle for opponents to prove
that. Experience shows that the best action is to offer some
other steps to be taken by the people under pressure to "do
something," steps they can take back to their constituents
and defend in a practical way.

The fourth quality of the new breed is the most general,
and it is related to the opening point about having to match
up to the values of society. The new breed has staying
power, I believe, because the people involved see their
objectives broadly. It is, of course, partly self-serving to look
for ways to work better with government. You do that to
make your company run better and thereby make more
profit. The corollary purpose, though, is to help make the
goverment work better and thereby make for a better society.

Thus you will find chief executives today working with
government on some matters far removed from their own
corporate interests—the Panama Canal treaty for example,
or the program to reform the Civil Service system, or the
problems of minority unemployment in urban centers where
their corporations do not have any plants.

It is hard to know where to draw the line. Unless they
are careful, executives can get sucked into controversial areas
where they don't have any particular competence, and in
extreme cases their efforts to help could amount to unwar-
ranted meddling. Yet at the same time, executives cannot
walk away from national and community problems on the
grounds that they don't have all the answers. Who does?

Those of us in business management and those who will
come into these jobs in the future have an obligation to
help where possible, recognizing our own limitations, but

realizing too that we can go a long way toward improving the climate between business and government, thus ending the ancient, mutually destructive, and unproductive animosity that has too long discolored the American political and economic environment.

4 The Educational Opportunity

JOHN T. DUNLOP

Lamont University Professor
Harvard University

I T IS PROBABLY not too much to say that business executives and government officials often do not get along. They do not understand each other; they do not hear or listen to each other; they do not appreciate the purposes or the constraints on each other. They are often highly suspicious of the other's motives. Their differences in age, compensation, perceptions of power and authority, and relations to the press and public processes are all factors exacerbating friction.

One prerequisite to constructive education among business and government executives and managers is, of course, professors, or pairs of professors, who are comfortable in both worlds. They cannot be so identified with one sphere, or so hostile to the other, or so rarefied and detached from both, that they cannot stimulate and lead both groups to interact frankly with a passion to learn and to understand an unknown or misperceived world. These professors need also to place the contemporary problems in our country in the setting of historical developments here and the arrangements of business and government abroad with the insights of Professor Alfred D. Chandler, Jr. (See Chapter 1).

Beyond the task of enhancing mutual understanding and civilized discourse, there is the educational opportunity to work on some difficult and exciting intellectual and practical problems.

There has long been thought to be a bias on the left bank of the Charles River, going downstream, (School of Government and Harvard College) toward aggregate public policies for the economy, toward governmental action as a ready means to correct perceived injustice or inequity and toward regarding itself as the intellectual arbiter of the public interest. At the same time, the right bank (with the Business School) has often been seen as having no vision or concern with societal issues, myopic in pursuing a thousand private decisions confronting the individual enterprise, with public policy being specified or given by others. Such caricatures of an earlier day are not descriptive or valid today, if they ever were. The Charles River is quite narrow today compared to the distance between the two sides forty years ago when I first came to Cambridge. The new location of the School of Government will contribute further to placing a strong hyphen between business and government in our programs.

There are at least three ways in which the inherited intellectual tools of our times, as they are applied to the formulation of governmental policies, and particularly public economic policies, need to be challenged and improved. First, we need a better understanding of the complex relations and interactions of the aggregate economy and the constituent sectors and parts. These inadequacies are reflected in our failures to understand and grapple with the issues of inflation and unemployment, persistent low productivity growth, paralyzing uncertainty in government regulations and the failure of our political processes to come to grips with overriding structural problems within decent intervals. We need, as George Shultz says in Chapter 2, a better appreciation of the relative roles of "doing" organizations and "debating" organizations.

Second, we need a better appreciation of the new interdependencies of the United States and the rest of the world and what is essential and nonessential for our security and prosperity in the real world and in real time. Domestic and foreign policies are increasingly creating one world.

Third, we need intellectual and analytical tools, beyond puzzle solving, which take greater account simultaneously of economic and political considerations in problem solving. Irving Shapiro has pointedly well said: ". . . you don't reach decisions in government the way an engineer [or, I may add, an economist] chooses the most efficient process for producing a product: In political life you don't 'optimize,' you compromise. Otherwise you don't get anything done."[1] In this spirit you will pardon my special perspective for holding that it is as important for a manager in the public arena or in private business for that matter, to practice the art of negotiations as to understand the theory of markets; the two are not entirely separate.

These and other intellectual questions are fundamental to several disciplines as well as central to hard, practical decisions in the business-government arena. These questions deserve to attract the best minds among our younger scholars —those with a flair for genuine accomplishments. These are not backwaters of the academic world, but the frontiers of reflection and action in a new respect for the private and public sectors.

In addition to enhancing mutual understanding and fac-

1. *Wall Street Journal,* May 30, 1978.

ing the intellectual challenges of business and government, there is the educational opportunity of providing in the university a continuing forum in which representatives of business and government, at policy-making levels, can meet with representatives of other groups such as organized labor and environmentalists, in association with certain knowledgeable academics, to consider specific problematic areas.

The academic atmosphere on occasion can provide a measure of quieting dispassion; it is relatively neutral turf, and it is somewhat away from the charged atmosphere of Washington without being remote. The development and discussion of a factual base, mutual agreement, or understanding and consensus on the facts, as every mediator or policy maker knows, is a major preliminary step in decomposing complex issues, reducing emotional and ideological content, defining problems, and considering alternate courses of action. The usefulness of a factual base is enhanced when the technical staff of all parties first can be brought into a wide measure of agreement on factual matters. In public policy making factual issues cannot simply be relegated to scientific experts; there must be a measure of consensus among responsible decision makers. The opportunity to educate and develop the background of a better informed press, at some stages of discussion in some situations, also needs to be explored.

The systematic explorations of specific areas of business and government interaction, on a continuing basis in a university, with policy makers from several camps, is an indispensable step in the development of more constructive national policies. Lest there be misunderstanding, two points need to be crystal clear. First, the university or school as an entity should take no position on these issues of policy; only individual professors may be related to their proposals or the proposals they help to develop. Second, these processes in no way displace any of the formal procedures of the executive or legislative branch. But an excessively litigious society, paralyzed by conflicting goals and a rapidly changing set of problems, needs to explore new ways to develop informed consensus and mutual accommodation. These aspirations require the development of new types of leaders in business, labor and government, as well as new types of professors, at home across all these organizations and in their interactions.

5 | The Business-Government Problem: Inherent Difficulties and Emerging Solutions

RICHARD G. DARMAN

Lecturer in Public Policy and Management
Graduate School of Government
Harvard University

LAURENCE E. LYNN, JR.

Professor of Public Policy
John F. Kennedy School of Government
Harvard University

ONCE, IT WAS SAID, the business of America was business. Not only was government small relative to the private sector, but businessmen apparently had the power to shift business-government relations in their favor.[1] In the 1920s, they stemmed the tide of Progressive Era reforms by supporting the election of pro-business Presidents and the appointment of business leaders to key government jobs by gaining approval of measures such as protective tariffs and by encouraging the transformation of the Federal Trade Commission from a central agency of government regulation to a warm supporter of business self-regulation. The active businessmen of this era were not, however, the "greedy capitalists" whose attitudes and actions

---

1. The terms "business," "businessmen," and "government" are somewhat misleading abstractions—masking at least as much diversity as similarity among their constituent elements. For the purpose of this essay, however, conventional associations with these terms will not prove fundamentally misleading.

inspired government regulations in the first place. Many
saw success in business as a service to society, not as merely
the pursuit of private gain. It was a leader in improving
business-government relations, Herbert Hoover, who in
1928 declared war on poverty.

Today, the business of America seems to many to be
government. Though an exaggeration, this statement is not
outlandish. Not only does government control a significant
share of national resources; its expenditure, regulatory, and
redistributive activities affect virtually every kind of private
transaction.

The growth of government has produced many benefits
in the "public interest"—for example, cleaner air and water,
more equitably distributed employment opportunities, consumer protection against hazards and frauds, a better liveli-
hood for the poor, even the preservation of a market-oriented
system otherwise threatened by its destructive tendencies
toward excess. Benefits have also been produced for "private
interests"—for example, the promotion of the aerospace and
solar energy industries, the protection of older domestic
sectors from disorderly foreign competition, and the fostering of growth in sectors related to government activity, such
as the practice of law and the production of equipment and
services for pollution clean-up.

The growth of government, however, has occurred in
significant part at the expense of the business sector. By
insuring people against economic risks; expanding the avail-
ability of public relief and social services; retaining or acquiring property rights in land and material resources;
protecting people against health and safety risks; and affecting the prices, quality, and quantity of goods and services
traded in private markets—not to mention by taxing economic activities—the government has brought about an allo-

cation of economic effort and rewards quite different from what business would endorse.

Businessmen would no doubt like to have the political influence business once had so that they could again shift business-government relations in their favor. Self-interest underlies this desire in part, as does the belief that a confident and responsibly managed private sector could solve many social problems more effectively than government. Complaints about business-government relations go well beyond ideological expressions or policy disagreements, however. In the characteristic business view, excessive intrusion into private decisions, bureaucracy, and uncertainty frustrate capital investment planning, productivity improvement, and research, thereby reducing the capacity of the private sector to generate jobs, products, and services. And in some business quarters, many government agencies are viewed as stupid (the Occupational Health and Safety Administration), insensitive (the Environmental Protection Agency, or incompetent (the Department of Energy).

The contrasting view, held by supporters and administrators of government activities affecting business, is that the pace and character of government growth since the Depression reflect responses to demonstrable failures on the part of business either to recognize or to accede to the public's stake in their activities. According to this view, business—especially large and powerful corporations—is fundamentally conservative and unprogressive. Despite clear evidence of the public's desire for a cleaner environment; safer good, services, and working conditions; and informative, honest advertising, business tends to respond only when required to by laws and regulations enforced by the courts. Moreover, the economic power of business is so great—as is its willingness to use it to frustrate measures the public wants—that government intervention in business decision making is mandatory if the public interest is to be served.

Both these views—the "business" view and the "government" view—have considerable limitations and considerable validity. Nonetheless, people who hold them are usually in sharp conflict. Both sectors want change: public officials and the interests that support them want reductions in the time and effort required to obtain responsible behavior by business; and businessmen want reductions in the uncertainty of government behavior and in the detailed interference by government in their decisions. The destructive effects generated by repeated collisions between these two points of view comprise the contemporary "business-government problem."

Even if the two sectors communicated well with each other, progress would be hard to achieve because the substantive issues that arise under the heading of business-government relations are inherently difficult. (How should we balance competing demands for clean air, reasonably priced automobiles, and fuel economy?) The two sectors do not communicate well, however, thus compounding the difficulties. One reason is cultural: business leaders are usually older, have higher incomes, and have different educational and career backgrounds than the public officials with whom they must deal. Businessmen's goals, decision-making styles, values, and social perspectives are different from those of the relatively young economists, lawyers, social activists, academics, and career civil servants on government or congressional staffs.[2] Another reason is political: business leaders

2. A recent Korn/Ferry International survey of 3,600 senior-level executives working at several hundred of the largest U.S. corporations found: The average senior VP has worked for the same company for nearly twenty years. The composite executive emerging from the survey is a fifty-three-year-old white male, educated at a large public university,

are responsible primarily to stockholders and only secondarily to their employees, union leaders, creditors, consumers, and public officials. In general, the primary responsibilities of public officials are to the voters and public, and are accordingly more diffuse, ambiguous, changeable, and controversial. A third reason is structural: in running their organizations, business leaders have relative freedom to set goals, marshal resources, and act. Public officials have far less discretion.

Thus the interests, concerns, and capacities to act of the two sectors, though they overlap, are not the same. Yet, legitimate differences are often viewed with suspicion and hostility by both sides. Stereotypes develop and are reinforced. Businessmen see government as incompetent and unpredictable. Public officials see businessmen as all too predictable and selfish. Communication deteriorates. The problem gets worse.

It is naive to believe that in the American "mixed" economy this problem can be "solved" or that radical changes in business-government relations are possible. Some changes are desirable, however, and they are possible if those with a stake in improved relations have a clearer understanding of what is wrong and of what can realistically be done about it. To help promote such understanding—and to point toward what *can* sensibly be done—is the purpose of this essay.

The business-government problem exists in a context in which the management of virtually all large organizations is becoming more complex. Both public and private mana-

---

a registered Republican, Protestant, father of three whose wife does not work outside the home, with a background in accounting or finance, and a belief that "hard work" rather than exceptional intelligence or creativity is the key to success. The contrast with government "whiz kids" or "activists," who routinely influence multibillion dollar decisions, could hardly be more stark.

gers have more things to think about, and their ability to accomplish what they set out to do is increasingly problematic. Recognition of the inherent difficulties of the public manager's problem, the private manager's problem, and their problem of dealing with each other, must underlie any effort to alleviate the "business-government problem." In pointing to what can sensibly be done, therefore, this essay also emphasizes these inherent difficulties.

The Problem of Public Management

By any measure, the size and complexity of government have grown rapidly and continuously in the past two decades. In business organizations facing expansion and diversification of markets and changes in technology, managerial responsibility has tended to become decentralized. Virtually the opposite occurs in governmental organizations; faced with change, responsibility and accountability move toward the top. Consumer dissatisfaction with a defective automobile often focuses on the salesman or the dealer; it is rarely directed at the chief executive officer. Consumer dissatisfaction with a social security or public assistance payment, in contrast, is seldom directed at the social worker; rather it is directed at the federal government or the Secretary of HEW. The energy crisis has generated anger at OPEC, the oil companies, and the President; but the scapegoat singled out most widely—the one whose head many people say should roll—is the Secretary of Energy. When a fatal airplane crash occurs, one seldom sees the president of the airline or the aircraft manufacturer or the chief federal safety inspector on television; one sees, and expects answers from, the head of the Federal Aviation Administration.

The consequences of size, complexity, and centralization take several forms. For the public manager the demands of the job are extraordinary. The time demands alone are remarkable. Most public managers have literally hundreds of programs, issues, and constituencies with a legitimate claim to merit serious concern. All require some of his or her time and attention, and most of them could easily absorb all of it. Dozens of subordinates, interest group representatives, legislators, other public officials, and representatives of the media request or demand this time and attention. The public manager can seldom afford to drop everything and concentrate on the crisis of the moment, yet to do less often seems risky and irresponsible. If a mistake is made, the President, the Congress, and the media will not blame the special assistant, or the assistant secretary, or the division director to whom responsibility might have been delegated. As suggested above, they will blame the top official. With this kind of pressure, it is small wonder that public managers seem insufficiently sensitive to the importance of tending business-government relations.

Although held accountable, public managers have minimal discretion in choosing their subordinates, in making decisions, and in directly controlling their organizations. A recent article in a national business magazine described how a company had systematically acquired weak and failing manufacturing enterprises and made them profitable by cutting the number of products in half, consolidating management operations, reducing staff by one-third, replacing weak managers, and introducing improved cost accounting down to the level of pencils and paperclips. The only one of these actions that a public manager in a similar situation could expect to take is to count pencils and paperclips; and the result would almost surely be a drop in morale and productivity that would swamp the savings.

To an increasing extent, a controversial exercise of discretion invites litigation, with unpredictable consequences.

Much of the tedious procedural detail that seems to be associated with governmental decision making is a product of the litigious environment in which public managers operate. "Legal sufficiency" has become an important management objective, a contributor to complexity, and a further irritant in many business-government relations. (A good example is the emergence of national policy toward nondeterioration of air quality.)

Further, public managers are assigned responsibility to perform tasks of incredible difficulty, in many cases to perform near-miracles. Public managers are held accountable for insuring that an adequate supply of energy is available to all regions, industries, and income groups; adequate housing is available to poor people; disadvantaged groups have access to higher education; fathers support their families; children are not poisoned or maimed by their toys; etc. These are tasks for which there are often no adequate technologies or know-how, no realistic notions as to costs, no measures of effectiveness, and no supportive consensus about either ends or means. No matter what the manager does, some politically powerful group will complain.

Even tasks that sound simple are complex. For example, suppose one is asked to establish policies by which the costs of prescription drugs are reimbursed under Medicaid and Medicare, a multibillion-dollar issue involving business-government relations. To what extent should one take into account the existence of patent monopolies, nonprice competition, the possibilities of overuse and misuse of drug therapies, inflation in therapeutic drug prices? If one could answer, "not at all," the problem might indeed be simple. But one cannot. Congress has clearly indicated its displeasure with the high profits earned by pharmaceutical manufacturers, excessively wide price variations among drugs of the same chemical composition, expenditures for drugs that are ineffective, and the excessive or inappropriate use of drugs for old and poor patients leading to hospitalization for drug toxicity. One proposal might be to reimburse at the lowest price charged for chemically identical drugs, but, experts will testify, chemical equivalence is not bioequivalance (similarity in rate and extent to which active ingredients are absorbed into the blood). Drug companies will testify that bioequivalence is not therapeutic equivalence. The Senate will hold hearings; the Office of Technology Assessment will do a study; two thousand comments on the proposal, mostly negative, will be received. The result is creation of a Pharmaceutical Reimbursement Board; a Pharmaceutical Reimbursement Advisory Committee; and detailed procedures involving findings, publication, review, and comment for dealing with each drug. (This is the "solution," incidentally, that was in fact arrived at by a fundamentally conservative HEW Secretary who is now a businessman.)

As the latter example makes clear, public managers are expected to devise ways of influencing or controlling business decisions so that they conform to the "public interest," whatever the political process may determine that to be. For example, public sentiment often favors controls on key prices such as gasoline and fuel oil, physicians' fees and the costs of drugs, transportation rates, and rents; controls on what is done with effluents, pollution emissions, and toxic wastes; the safety of airplanes, nuclear power plants, and mass transit systems; and so on down a very long list. In reaching decisions on such issues, public managers cannot freely choose the philosophy, goals, or instruments of government action—as if analysis of "the merits" could be separated from legitimate expressions of political and value choice. Unless protected by powerful congressional backers, as the Joint Committee on Atomic Energy once protected the Atomic Energy Commission, public managers cannot be probusiness if the political context dictates otherwise. Let the automobile manufacturers or the public utilities receive a favorable decision from the EPA administrator and opponents will immediately act to tighten the laws and seek more specific and binding regulations.

Public managers are found, in short, to be held accountable for the performance of extraordinarily difficult tasks, under extreme pressures, with inadequate technology and resources, in the pursuit of politically determined objectives that will frequently run counter to many private interests. It should be little wonder that they are, in many quarters, viewed with disfavor.

The Problem for Private Management

"Disfavor" is often too temperate an adjective to describe the businessman's reaction to government. Among private managers the dominant reaction to government growth has been dismay, often bordering on outrage. To them, greater governmental intervention has typically created more problems than it has solved.

Government's pervasive role has made it a fundamental variable influencing the outcome of major corporate investment decisions. Particular governmental policy decisions— that is, above and beyond general fiscal, monetary, and income security policy decisions—now directly determine or heavily influence roughly 40 percent of new capital investment (compared with roughly 5 percent two decades ago).[3] Given the importance of government to the corporate en-

3. Recent studies of aggregate private cost and investment effects of government policy decisions have tended to focus on incremental regulatory compliance costs, and have produced numbers about one-third as high as those used here. The measure suggested here—"directly determine or heavily influence"—is, of course, significantly broader than the direct, measurable, incremental regulatory compliance costs.

vironment, private managers are hardly comforted by the fact that public policy making is complex and uncertain, and getting more so.

This point is made clear by considering any of a vast number of major decision problems from a private manager's perspective. One might consider whether to invest hundreds of millions of front-end dollars in a multibillion-dollar pipeline project involving uncertainties with respect to requirements for environmental protection and restoration, routing, construction standards, capital costs, rates, and competition; whether to reinvest in domestic production of a product threatened by a potential policy decision to liberalize trade preferences for certain developing countries; whether to invest in nonmilitary high technology development when access to export markets could be restricted because of foreign policy considerations; and so on.

The problem of government-induced uncertainty is compounded when one considers a distinctive quality of many governmental decisions. They tend to amount to yes-no decisions—permit export or not, allow market entry or not, set an inflexible standard, etc.—and the outcome often exceeds the make-or-break point for affected business. The prospect, then, from the private manager's perspective, is not only one of considerable and extended uncertainty, but also one of major down-side risk.

Because government-induced uncertainty is pervasive, it has developed into a general management concern. The function of influencing and adapting to government policy uncertainties has, accordingly, become a significant responsibility of general management. Indeed, in the past two decades, the "governmental affairs" function has been *the* principal new responsibility added to top corporate management's traditional functional concerns.

Nonetheless, the challenge of managing governmental

affairs effectively remains, by and large, to be met. Part of the problem derives from the inherent difficulties of performing governmental affairs functions in today's environment. The task of predicting public policy decisions in a timely fashion, for example, is complicated. Legislative and regulatory monitoring services typically provide information at too late a stage in the policy development process to be of strategic value. "Eyes and ears" reporting services and the newer computerized document analysis and opinion survey services provide somewhat greater lead time for analysis, but their products are still only raw material for a more sophisticated synthesis that requires a combination of sociopolitical analysis, bureaucratic analysis, and an indepth understanding of the substance of issues.

The related task of analyzing the effects of potential public policy decisions is as difficult for the private manager as it is for his or her public couterpart. Consider, for example, any of the public policy choices referred to above. Their effects are complex and highly difficult to assess. For the private manager, the analytic task is complicated further by the fact that aggregate estimates, which are often sufficient for the public manager, are typically insufficient for the private manager. A private manager needs to know the effects on his or her firm relative to its competition; government intervention almost always changes the competitive position of firms within an industry.

The classical task of influencing public policy decisions is undergoing an important transformation. A combination of sociopolitical forces has increased "government in the sunshine," opened up access to decision-making processes, and added to the formal constraints upon public-private relationships. One significant effect of these developments has been even more litigation in an already highly litigious society. Interest groups, third, fourth, and fifth parties now have greater substantive basis and procedural opportunity to contest public policy development and, at a minimum, to slow down the policy development processes. A second significant effect has been growing attention to argument on the merits as a model of influence. Yet, because public policy problems are complex, because definitive data is rarely available, and because relevant interests are often in conflict, persuasive argument on the merits is inherently difficult. The net effect, from the private perspective, is not only reduced influence, but greater uncertainty.

Furthermore, the traditional training and experience of private managers provides inadequate preparation for performance or oversight of the new, more demanding, governmental affairs functions. Private sector approaches to marketing are less than wholly applicable to "consumers" of public policy, who are skeptical of corporate sponsorship and perceive a significant divergence between their interests and corporate interests. Private sector experience with finance and production engineering can be misleading— insofar as it may lead managers to expect that decisions can be made on the basis of reliable cost information, pilot-scale testing, operations research analysis, and a shared interest in the "bottom line." The corporate "public affairs" perspective has typically been oriented toward "public relations," rather than toward systematic public policy analysis and effective argument on the merits. Although corporate legal experience often involves exposure to public policy, it has characteristically been oriented toward static legal risk analysis before the fact, and toward the judicial and quasi-judicial processes of administrative rule making or formal litigation after the fact.

Remedying these weaknesses may entail significant shifts in corporate power relationships. Staff offices responsible for public affairs, governmental affairs, law, and planning are

not viewed as major corporate power centers or as routes
to the top. Indeed, in many corporations these offices are
viewed with a cultural prejudice against "overhead" that
ranges from skepticism to contempt. The notion of increasing overhead can be expected to meet some resistance in any
case (even though the dollars involved may represent a very
small percentage of total costs.) The resistance is likely to
be compounded if a reallocation of power is involved.

For all these reasons, then, managing governmental affairs has become highly problematic. It is understandable
that notwithstanding the fundamental importance of public
policy—and allowing for the belated recognition that coping
with it is an inescapable necessity—most corporations are
still in an early stage of adaptation to this new management
challenge.

The Mutual Problem:
Managing Business-Government Relations

Regardless of their differences, the public and private sectors have important interests in common. These common
interests are not yet fully perceived or treated as such. They
must be, however, if progress is to be made in addressing
business-government problems in a practical and responsible
way. Indeed, mutual recognition and pursuit of these interests may be essential to the preservation of a democratic,
market-oriented system.

These interests—that should be understood as common
interests—include: (1) increasing public confidence in the
integrity and fairness of public policy decision processes; (2)
keeping the burden of public responsibilities within manageable bounds; (3) reducing the irrational portion of the
(partly rational) adversarialism that has characterized
American business-government relations; and (4) increasing the intelligence and sophistication with which (a) the

public sector manages its growing responsibilities, and (b) the private sector manages its response to the uncertainty this new governmental responsibility creates.

The first interest—assuring the fairness and integrity of public policy decision making—has not received consistent and serious attention from either sector. Recently, concerns for greater equity have led to increased opportunities for affected parties to gain access to judicial and quasi-judicial processes. Concerns identified by the catch-phrase "post-Watergate morality" have stimulated a flurry of attention across several fronts: freedom-of-information and "sunshine" requirements, lobbying disclosure requirements, proscription of certain payments to foreign officials, domestic campaign finance reform, and the "Ethics in Government Act." However, reforms intended to increase fairness and integrity may also tend to decrease the flexibility, efficiency, and effectiveness of public-private exchanges. "Opening" to public view and formalizing the processes of exchange have led some parties to be less forthcoming, and tightening the conflict-of-interest requirements are said to have discouraged many private individuals from entering public life. The challenge is to improve the quality of public-private exchange without sacrificing fairness and integrity.

The second interest—keeping the burden of public responsibilities within manageable bounds—is a traditional focus of business-government argument. It has won new allies in the public sector. Phased deregulation of the oil and gas sectors has been enacted; deregulation of the transportation sector has been advanced with at least as much public support as private; a Democratic administration and Congress have seriously expressed intentions to balance the budget; several states and localities have enacted, or are actively considering, tax and spending ceilings; and a majority of state legislatures have passed resolutions endorsing a Constitutional amendment intended to assure a balanced federal budget. These, along with the growing literature of doubt about governmental effectiveness, are symptoms of a growing awareness of the need for limits upon governmental growth.

To the extent that limits are in fact imposed, they may allow some stabilization of the public-private balance and an opportunity to reduce public-private strains. At the same time, however, one must note that some approaches to limiting government may have unintended side effects. A focus on government budgets runs the risk of forcing the further extension of governmental reach by increasing reliance on the "off-budget" redirection of private resources—through regulatory growth, as, for example, in the conspicuous case of national health policy. Limiting local spending and taxation risks increased centralization of governmental authority —as California's experience with Proposition 13 might suggest. The second interest, then, like the first, requires more sensitive attention than it has yet received if improvements in public-private relationships are to be achieved.

The third interest—reducing the irrational component, the exaggerated, inflexible posturing of the adversarial relationship—has received even less attention than the first two. However, there have been a few successes. Two are sometimes viewed as models worthy of replication: a cooperative advisory model, such as that used in the development of policy for the multilateral trade negotiations, and a model of mediation and public-private negotiation, such as that used in the development of U.S. policy with regard to the secondary Arab boycott of Israel.[4] There is also a related, if

4. The intensely contested U.S. policy debate concerning the Arab secondary boycott was resolved only when representatives of the administration, leading U.S. Jewish groups, and the Business Roundtable met for an extensive series of private mediating-negotiating sessions. This is referred to in the chapter by Irving Shapiro, a participant. For

less clear, symptom of private sector interest in reduced adversarialism: the increased contacts between chief executive officers and government officials in the presentation and negotiation of public policy positions. This involvement of chief executive officers is to be distinguished from the more traditional use of hired intermediaries, who as a practical matter are often less suited for this role because they have limited authority to make decisions.

It is important to emphasize that these signs of moderation in public-private conflict are limited. Successful applications of advisory and mediation models have been rare. And the increased participation of chief executive officers in governmental affairs functions—with a concomitant increase in flexible argument on the merits—has generally been limited to a small number of corporations (most visibly, those associated with the Business Roundtable). By and large, the tendency of government policy makers to exclude or disregard business interests and the corresponding tendency of business to offer only inflexible briefs on behalf of narrow interests are all too familiar.

The fourth interest—becoming more intelligent in the performance of, and adaptation to, new government-policy-related responsibilities—is demonstrably appropriate, but not yet widely shared. In the public sector, it has been reflected in the development and application of increasingly sophisticated techniques of policy analysis, in the growing attention to economic values in the balancing of competing objectives, and in a new appreciation of economic incentives in the de-

---

a more detailed analysis, see the special issue of the *Georgia Journal of International and Comparative Law*, "The Arab Boycott and the International Response" (vol. 8, 1978). Even with this constructively mediated policy process, the resulting legislation and regulation is highly complex—as is detailed in the Ludwig and Smith article (*op. cit.*), "Morality Plus Pragmatism Equals Complexity."

sign of policies. It has also been reflected in the evolution of systematic approaches to the management of policy development—although it is important to note that these management reforms have generally *not* addressed the issue of improving the government's capacity to involve private management constructively in the policy development process.

In the private sector, particularly among large corporations, the interest in becoming more intelligent with respect to public policy has been shown in several ways. The most obvious way has been the direct recruitment to the ranks of top management (not just to Washington offices) of individuals with extensive government experience, though this route has been followed in only a limited number of cases. Of more general relevance has been the recent experimentation with new systems and structures for the treatment of public issues. This is reflected, for example, in the rise of "environmental scanning" and "emerging issue" analysis. These new functions (or old functions performed more systematically with respect to public policy) serve to identify—well in advance of their rigid crystallization—public policy issues that may be of special, perhaps even strategic, importance to the corporation. Increasingly, such issues are monitored for appropriate action by one form or another of corporate "governmental affairs committee," with high-level membership drawn from across the corporation. In some large corporations, "issue managers" (generally drawn from within the governmental affairs office) are given broad coordinative responsibility for the management of corporate policy development with regard to particularly important issues. Notwithstanding these developments, however, the staff resources routinely allocated to internal analysis of public policy-related issues (or to the management and utilization of such analysis performed externally) remains relatively thin in all but a few companies. Further, both the intellectual connections and the internal bureaucratic connections between public issue analysis and main-line corporate planning and decision making remain characteristically weak.[5]

Directions for Further Change

In this brief essay, it is not possible to examine in detail the directions for further adaptation of the American business-government relationship—to "solve," in any complete sense, the "business-government problem." It is possible, however, to outline the directions in which partial solutions may be found, while noting also the rough boundaries beyond which practicable solutions are unlikely to extend.

The first two interests would seem to require some tempering. The legal framework for the protection of fairness and integrity has now been well developed. There remains the challenge of assuring continuous and vigorous enforcement of the rights and duties this framework defines. It is the view of the authors that the present framework imposes a burden upon public-private exchange that is bearable and, on balance, worth paying; an emphasis on enforcement of existing law is now preferable to the further expansion of the legal framework itself; and that further expansion of the framework could not only distract enforcement efforts but be counterproductive. (This point is most obviously suggested by the recent interest in addressing the conflict-of-interest problem through what would amount to the regulation of career paths, rather than through vigorous enforcement of disclosure, divestiture, and recusal requirements—reducing

5. For a recent overview survey of current corporate approaches to the management of public issues, see P. S. McGrath, *Redefining Corporate-Federal Relations,* and J. K. Brown, *The Business of Issues: Coping with the Company's Environments,* Conference Board Reports nos. 757 and 758, respectively (1979).

public-private job mobility and, thereby, expanding the already excessive cultural gap between the public and private sectors.)

The interest in limiting the growth of government must also be tempered by realism. The growth of government may be slowed or even stabilized, but it is virtually certain not to be reversed. Aggregate U.S. governmental expenditures taken as a percentage of gross national product remain below the levels of most developed societies, and the opportunities for shrinking are few. Indeed, it may be that in an increasingly affluent society, claims of "rights" requiring public subsidy will generally increase as fast as the capacity to meet them.

Above and beyond claims for subsidy, the demands for regulatory protection from the risks and secondary effects of increasing technological development show no significant signs of abatement. The problems involved typically have characteristics of "externality" that even market-oriented economists would argue require some governmental intervention in order to be effectively addressed. The movement toward "deregulation" of certain industries subject to traditional economic regulation is, in this context, not to be confused with the character and condition of issues involving environmental protection, health, and safety (for which, to emphasize the point, one might read toxic wastes or the ozone layer, carcinogens or cotton dust, and Three Mile Island or DC-10s). In the latter areas, "regulatory reform" has some chance of meaning "more intelligent regulations," but no reasonable prospect of meaning "deregulation."

In considering the need to temper the interest in governmental limitation with a degree of realism, there is a further point to be emphasized: the prospects for progress with respect to the third and fourth interests (less adversarialism and greater intelligence) may depend on the extent to which this second interest is kept in reasonable perspective. Or, to put the matter the other way around, as long as an image of the possible reversibility of the recent growth of government survives, the necessary adaptations to the inescapable realities of pervasive governmental influence are likely to be postponed.

Happily, the third interest—reducing the irrational component of the present adversarialism—offers some promise. The objective is more than aesthetic (to improve the tone of relationships). It is also substantive and practical, for excessive adversarialism tends to have an adverse effect upon both public and private interests. It discourages the exchange of information. It encourages overattention to polar positions and underanalysis of intermediate alternatives—notwithstanding the fact that intermediate alternatives are often fashioned (clumsily) as last minute "compromises." It tends to be self-reinforcing: bad experience seems to justify the behavior pattern that produces more bad experience.

What would be preferable is less easy to accomplish than to state: an environment in which points of difference and agreement on facts, methodologies, judgments, and values can be clarified and distinguished, and in which plausible and responsible policy options can be fully and fairly analyzed. The most serious obstacle to achieving this is the problem of breaking the self-reinforcing cycle of distrust and finding a mechanism to engage the parties flexibly and constructively. This is difficult in any case of human or institutional relations. It is particularly difficult when (as in the case of business-government relations) the interests of the parties are, in some respects, inherently in conflict.

Apart from the few exceptions noted above, the parties—particularly the public sector parties—are not yet even seriously trying to build constructive relationships. The reasons for this are many. They are partly cultural and partly legal (as suggested above). They are also partly personal: many

individuals are neither comfortable with nor expert at mediative roles. Some feel public-private relationships threaten
purity; most feel too pressed for time. Nonetheless, there
are several different lines of constructive adaptation that are
feasible and that merit further development. These lines of
possible adaptation have in common a greater degree of
prior consultation among concerned parties than is now
characteristic.

One such line is in the direction of more widespread use
of formal and informal models of mediation and negotiation.
This approach has been used most extensively with respect
to labor-management issues involving the public interest.
But, as suggested by the Arab boycott example, it has far
greater potential. It requires highly sophisticated mediator-
negotiators, a scarce resource. Yet it is important to note that
the mediative role does not have to be confined to government officials; indeed, there may be significant undeveloped
opportunities for constructive intermediation under private
auspices (including academic auspices).[6]

There are, however, significant limits on the possible extension of a negotiation-mediation model. The model, in
order to be workable, generally requires that a small number
of individuals engage in the negotiating or quasi-negotiating
processes, and that they do so in private. This means that the
individuals involved must have the authority and capacity to
represent the constituent interests involved. For many complex public policy problems, the range of concerned interests
is so wide (and, often, the associated power structure is so
fragmented) that the negotiation-mediation model cannot

6. Harvard University is in the experimenting stage of developing an
improved mediative capability for policy development—through a program of "Executive Sessions," as alluded to in the chapter above by
John T. Dunlop. (For further details, see R. G. Darman, "Harvard
Executive Session," February 1979.)

effectively be applied. Or rather, the form of the model to be applied becomes the U.S. Congress, an institution well-suited for value judgment, but less well-suited for the prior organization and clarification of issues. Indeed, in virtually any significant case, mediative efforts may be limited by the need to withstand congressional scrutiny (for conformity with legislative intent) or congressional action (for implementing authority and resources). Notwithstanding these limits, however, there is still a large class of issues that could benefit from a mediative approach to policy development.

A second constructive line of adaptation could seek to make more effective use of the hundreds of public advisory committees that now serve principally as window dressing, particularly since they have been made more representative. The favorable example of the use of the MTN advisory system is a rare one, but not unique.[7] It was, admittedly, made possible because the political power of the interests involved and the legislation establishing the advisory structure combined to create a powerful incentive for the executive branch to take the advisory structure seriously. (The incentive was the prospect of otherwise losing an up-down congressional vote on implementing legislation.) But it is arguable that such incentives exist (although less formally so) for most complex public policy issues. And the executive branch itself, as well as the public and private interests involved, might therefore be better served by more serious attention to at least some portions of the elaborate public advisory structure that already exists.

7. Other examples of effective advisory committee participation might include U.S. policy development with respect to the O.E.C.D. "Declaration on Guidelines for Multinational Enterprises, National Treatment, International Investment Incentives and Disincentives, and Consultation Procedures" (1976) and U.S. policy development with respect to law of the sea (1973–present). Examples are not only relatively few, but they tend to be disproportionately associated with foreign policy.

A final, and related, line of adaptation could extend certain executive branch reforms recently applied in the public sector management of complex policy development, in order to allow greater inclusion of private sector perspectives in general policy development (that is, in processes not regulated by the Administrative Procedures Act). These little noticed and only intermittently practiced reforms have included, in particular, management techniques to assure internal due process and the balanced representation of relevant bureaucratic interests. Their selective extension to include private interests could now be informally undertaken in ways that are fair, relatively efficient, and manageable.[8]

The fourth interest—increased public-private intelligence and sophistication with respect to each other—also offers some promise of further constructive adaptation. In the public sector, the most obvious initiatives under this heading are those widely associated with "regulatory reform" (understood to mean sensible regulation more often than deregulation). These initiatives range from the greater use of economic incentives, to the refinement of guidelines for the

8. The reforms in the management of federal policy development alluded to herein include: improved process control systems (through the intelligent use of executive secretaries and policy coordination mechanisms); improved systems of constructive check-and-balance among competing policy advocates (see A. George, "The Case for Multiple Advocacy in Foreign Policy Making," *American Political Science Review,* 1972, and R. Porter, *The Economic Policy Board* [forthcoming]); and improved systems for the comprehensive management of major agency policy development (see L. Lynn and J. M. Seidl, " 'Bottom-Line' Management for Public Agencies," *Harvard Business Review* [January–February 1977]). These mechanisms lend themselves readily to the controlled and constructive inclusion of extra-governmental perspectives. There are, of course, limits set by needs to assure secrecy in some foreign policy development. As a general matter, the exclusion of extra-governmental participants on grounds of need for haste, secrecy, or "surprise" is often false, misguided, or unnecessary.

assessment of risks and their weighting in relation to costs and benefits, to analysis of aggregate regulatory impacts, to "regulatory budgeting," to such simple and straightforward administrative procedures as facilitating concurrent review of regulatory actions that might otherwise be sequential. The movement toward such "regulatory reasonableness" has been gaining momentum in the past six years. There remains the hard work of translating increased agreement-in-principle into satisfactory implementation. Fortunately, the climate in which this is to be done is dramatically more sensitive to the importance of economic interests than it was a decade ago.

In the private sector, the climate for more sophisticated and intelligent analysis is also improving. Simply as a function of natural succession, a new generation of corporate managers is rising—with fewer direct memories of a world in which government was not pervasive. Although this may mean some regrettable loss in the once vital free-enterprise spirit, it may also mean somewhat greater realism in the management of government affairs. This, as well as the growing government-related experience of present managers, should allow a relatively rapid extension of the internal corporate reforms noted above: particularly, systematic linkage of the newly developing corporate capacities for public issue identification and analysis with the functions of strategic policy development and implementation.

All this is not to suggest that the U.S. may be on the verge of abandoning the pattern of public-private conflict it has developed so highly in the past hundred years—abandoning it, perhaps, for its own variant of a "Japan Incorporated." Time horizons will continue to differ—with the private sector oriented toward a middle-range future, the period necessary to recover investment at a satisfactory rate of annual return and with the public sector oriented toward a peculiar combination of the long-range and the immediate. Substantive interests will, of course, also continue to differ, as will the capacity to address them. The government will be concerned with many aggregate effects that private interests will be less willing, or less able, to address; and the government will tend to have a greater capacity and inclination to analyze issues across a range of interrelated interests, many of which will tend to be beyond the ordinary analytic scope of a single firm or even an industry. These differences in orientation will mean continued differences in views of the merits. Further, notwithstanding improvements in the present adversarial climate, these differences will not easily be mediated. The capacity of private sector leaders to moderate their views will be limited somewhat by a combination of negotiators' prudence and an interest in preserving the appearance of a relatively wide base of support—forcing some "reduction to the lowest common denominator." Many of the choices and alternatives, however well analyzed, will remain inescapably difficult to make or to accept.

For all these reasons, then, the "business-government problem" must be addressed with a sensitive appreciation of its inherent difficulties. The problem can be alleviated to some significant degree; there is both opportunity for, and a reasonable prospect of, some limited adaptation to the realities of an environment in which public-private interaction has dramatically increased. But the problem can hardly be expected to disappear. Indeed, the challenge of managing business-government relations constructively—in the irreversibly "mixed" American system—is likely to continue its rise in importance on the public and private agendas.

6 | Educational Challenges in Teaching Business-Government Relations

Timken Professor of Business Administration
Harvard Business School

T HIS SMALL VOLUME is dedicated to a major future academic endeavor: a joint effort of two of Harvard's professional schools to explore the growing, yet elusive, phenomenon of business-government relations. Harvard's strategy in confronting this challenge is distinctive. While most other leading academic institutions have chosen to combine public and private management within the same professional school, Harvard has its distinct schools of public and business administration, with separate constituencies, faculties, and curricula. Each school retains its focus in terms of strategic mission. While recognizing the virtue and power of specialization, Harvard's emerging strategy also stresses the importance of integration. The University-wide program in Public Policy, and particularly the efforts of John Dunlop in the area of Business and Public Policy, are specifically aimed at this goal. It involves the appointment of at least two tenured professors, one at the School of Government (Public Policy Program) and one at the Business School, to work together as a coordinated team with supporting staff and resources. As stated by Dunlop:

> The separate but coordinated character of the appointments is fundamental to these proposals. It is essential that one of the senior persons be a regular member of the Business School faculty, and the other a regular member of the School of Government. These separate appointments are in no way likely to diminish their cooperation and joint activities; indeed, their combined effectiveness with the academic community and outside will be significantly enhanced by the proposed arrangements. In this sense, one or two joint appointments might not be nearly as effective, since professors holding such appointments do not always have the influence enjoyed by full-time members of a school's faculty.

Integration, therefore, does not occur in a vacuum. It does not rely on some superprofessor who is a master of two separate fields. Rather, it is built on each pillar of the bridge solidly rooted on each side of the river but also spanning it through a coordinated and major effort.

Integration of the Business and the Public Policy Programs must be rooted in respect for each other's different mission and uniqueness as well as in an understanding of what each professional school has accomplished and intends to pursue.

Within the context of this strategy, it is appropriate to review some academic history of the Business School's recent efforts of dealing with the business-government interface and to draw some lessons from it that may be applicable to the forthcoming joint effort between the Kennedy School of Government and the Business School. These efforts of the Business School have to be reviewed within the context of the institution and its available resources. By academic standards, the Harvard Business School is both a large and a diverse professional school. The size of its faculty and student body is substantial, and the scope of its programs and activities is broad. As in any other large diversified organization, strategic change became not solely an intellectual exercise but also an organizational and administrative challenge.

Alfred Chandler, in *Strategy and Structure*,[1] describes the transition of U.S. corporations from a functional centralized to a divisional decentralized form of organization. This major change in organization structure resulted from the need to manage the greater diversity and complexity that resulted from strategic moves toward more innovation and broader diversification. This organizational transition brought with it the requirement of a large number of general managers to run the newly decentralized divisions. The previously prevailing functional organization, in contrast, was built around specialists. Thus, the change in organization structure brought with it a need for management development. The newly required general managers could not be hired from the outside; they had to be obtained by converting functional specialists to a new role and different outlook.

The challenge confronting academic institutions that are serious about business-government relations is similar. It stands in stark contrast to other strategic changes implemented at leading business schools during the last few decades. For example, business schools undertook major efforts to place greater emphasis on mathematical decision theory or on behavioral sciences. In each instance, both fields were well developed by outstanding academicians with national reputations. These behavioral scientists as well as mathematicians were invited to join business school faculties. The Harvard Business School took an active part in this effort

1. Alfred D. Chandler, Jr., *Strategy and Structure: Chapters in the History of the Industrial Enterprise* (Cambridge, Mass.: MIT Press), 1962.

and was fortunate to "acquire," among others, Howard Raiffa and the current Dean, Larry Fouraker. For business-government relations, in contrast, the acquisition strategy does not work. There are no academic programs established precisely for this purpose, nor are there doctoral programs turning out this new breed of prospective faculty. Just as the first business organizations had to develop their own general managers, business schools embarking on the business-government interface have to develop their own faculty.

In order to implement this new approach, there was a need to attract a substantial number of generalists coming from a variety of backgrounds. This posed a particularly delicate problem in an academic setting where promotions are subject to collective review by the tenured faculty. In this setting, what are the chances of a generalist without roots in any of the traditional constituencies attempting to make a contribution in a field which is only emerging, enormously broad and elusive to simple exact analysis? Not surprisingly, the career path is one of high risk.

Given the hurdles to be overcome on the "people" dimension, the organizational structuring of the business-government activities became a critical variable. A certain similarity existed with the international business activities which were greatly expanded some two decades ago. The perennial issue for international business was whether to constitute it as a separate "area" (the equivalent of a department in other academic settings) or to incorporate it into the existing areas. Under the latter alternative, each area would have its international course(s) and other activities, such as research. Thus, the finance area would "internationalize" its required course and also offer an international finance course, a pattern which would be paralleled in most other areas. This latter approach clearly would most effectively foster an international orientation of the entire curriculum, but it would come at the expense of achieving the necessary critical mass by pooling the efforts of those faculty interested in international business. Instead, each international business faculty member would be immersed primarily in his other area and only secondarily in international business activities. Furthermore, being a minority of one in an area might limit the person's influence on the area's curriculum and research. The School's experience in international business pointed to success where sufficient critical mass was brought to bear, such as Ray Vernon's multinational research project[2] or the international business activities in the Doctoral Program. In the teaching program, on the other hand, the record was mixed, as it was difficult under the multi-area structure to devote sufficient resources consistently to the development and maintenance of the various international business courses.

Thus, both the prior experience in international business and the emerging nature of business-government relations pointed to the desirability of concentrating the new activities within a single area. In fact, there already existed such an area, called Business, Government and Society (BGS). BGS, however, was more an area in form than in substance, more a loose confederation of individual specialists than an integrated team. Its members came primarily from backgrounds in economics, law, and history; and many had public-policy experience themselves. Most were research-oriented and produced a small library of speeches, expert testimony, working papers, articles, doctoral theses, and books with the focus on the regulatory environment and business-government relationships.[3]

2. See Raymond Vernon, *Storm Over the Multinationals: The Real Issues* (Cambridge, Mass.: Harvard University Press), 1977.
3. Notable among these works were those of Paul W. Cherington on the regulation of airlines, the merchant marine, and television broadcasting, as well as his pioneering study *The Business Representative in*

The BGS area was responsible for the development and teaching of a number of MBA courses. Its mainstay was the required first-year course, *Environmental Analysis for Management* (EAM), which had gone through several name changes. First offered after World War II under the title of *Public Relationships and Responsibilities,* it was subsequently called *Business Responsibility in the American Society, The Manager in the American Economy,* and *Planning and the Business Environment.* There is a saying at the School that when a course frequently changes its name, it is in trouble. EAM was such a course.

Throughout its history its purpose was "to familiarize the student with the economic-legal-political-social environment within which business decisions are made and the business process takes place, the impact of such environmental factors on the shaping of business decisions, and the impact of such

---

Washington (1962). Raymond A. Bauer's work on social responsibility produced such monographs as *Social Indicators* (1966) and *The Corporate Social Audit* (1972), the latter with Dan H. Fenn, Jr. Another pioneering project, directed by Paul W. Cherington, produced *The Weapons Acquisitions Process: An Economic Analysis* by Merton J. Peck and Frederick M. Scherer (1962), *The Weapons Acquisitions Process: Economic Incentives* by Scherer (1964), and *Arming America: How the U.S. Buys Weapons* by J. Ronald Fox (1974). David L. Birch was the principal investigator for a large-scale investigation of urban policy making summarized in *The Businessman and the City* (1967) and *Patterns of Urban Change: The New Haven Experience* (1974). Lewis M. Schneider's *Marketing Urban Mass Transit* (1965) and *The Future of the U.S. Domestic Air Freight Industry* (1973) explored two highly regulated situations as did Kurt Borchardt's *Structure and Performance of the U.S. Communications Industry: Government Regulation and Company Planning* (1970). George C. Lodge's *The New American Ideology* (1975) analyzed the philosophical roots of "free enterprise," and Arthur M. Johnson's *Petroleum Pipelines and Public Policy* (1967) remains one of the best historical and economic case studies of a regulated industry. Johnson generalized his findings in *Government-Business Relationships: A Pragmatic Approach to the American Experience* (1965).

business decisions on the economy itself." Even though this description sounds quite contemporary, it is taken from the 1959–1960 catalogue. The required first-year course gave business-government relationships a central position. MBA students were given basic introductions to the national economic and social policy-making process as it involved the private sector and to the roles and tasks of such regulatory agencies as the Antitrust Division of the Department of Justice, the Interstate Commerce Commission, the Securities and Exchange Commission, the National Labor Relations Board, the Environmental Protection Agency, the Federal Trade Commission, the Federal Reserve Board, the Federal Communications Commission, the Federal Power Commission, and the Civil Aeronautics Board. This was accomplished through case studies and computer-based simulations of actual business firms interacting with public agencies. In the course, such public-private issues as productivity, employment, environmental quality, equal opportunity, inflation and energy were pursued with vigor. There was also special emphasis on business-government relations in the urban environment.[4]

It was not in defining the issues that the course encountered trouble but in its execution. It tried to cover too many different topics. Also, part of the problem was conceptual. As stated by George Lodge, who was associated with the course for many years, "we were boggled by the difficulty of integrating the many bits and pieces of the environment so as to be able to analyze it coherently and to realize the

4. The concepts and case materials of these courses were embodied in three textbooks which are still widely used: Paul W. Cook, Jr., *Cases in Antitrust Policy* (1964); Cook and George von Peterffy, *Problems of Corporate Power* (1966); and James P. Baughman, George C. Lodge, and Howard W. Pifer, *Environmental Analysis for Management* (1974).

interrelationships which tie it together." The experience with EAM is a common one: it is easy to postulate that important, multifaceted issues be taught, but it is extraordinarily difficult to execute such a project successfully. The gap between formulation and implementation of ideas is very wide indeed.

Where a course is difficult to teach because of the multiplicity of aspects and the open-endedness of the issues that it covers, it becomes a graveyard for junior faculty if it lacks a solid conceptual framework. The reason is simple. Without a rigorous framework, the course becomes the expression of the personality of the teacher. Experienced, skillful, and strong-willed senior faculty are able to impose their mark on the class and hold the course together through a combination of teaching skill and personality. But many younger faculty, lacking both confidence and skill and still having to learn the secrets of successful pedagogy, are not able to integrate the many difficult pieces. As a result, the student frequently sees nothing but chaos. Not surprisingly, EAM was viewed by nontenured faculty as a very high-risk career track.

In addition to EAM, the BGS area consisted of a number of second-year elective courses. Their common denominator was that they were taught by highly distinguished senior faculty. One such course was developed and taught by the late Paul Cherington under the title of *The Business Administrator and Government Policy*. Twenty years ago its course description stated: "This course deals with the relations between business and government from the point of view of the business administrator. It rests upon the assumption that government at the local, state, and federal levels will continue to play an important economic and social role and that businessmen, willingly or unwillingly, consciously or unconsciously, affect and in turn are affected by government policy and action and by politics." Another course was developed and taught by the late George Albert Smith under the title of *Business, Society and the Individual.* The 1959–1960 catalogue stated: "The main objectives of this course are to develop perspective, to encourage students to try to envision proper ends and means of business in our society, to oblige them to test their own senses of values, to afford practice in the often difficult art of resolving conflicts between the proper economic objectives of a particular enterprise and the fundamental goals of society." Another giant, who belonged to the BGS area, was the late Raymond Bauer, who, for example, in 1971–1972 taught a *Seminar on Policy Problems of Nonbusiness Institutions* with the following course description: "Primary emphasis in this seminar will be placed on those institutions of the public sector which impinge most directly on business. This means an intensive concentration on government institutions primarily on the federal and secondly on the state and local level." Last, but not least, BGS was the home of the distinguished Isidor Straus Professor of Business History, a chair most recently held by the late Ralph W. Hidy and his successor, Alfred D. Chandler. Hidy and Chandler taught the traditional second-year course in *Business History* in which "emphasis is given to interaction between business activities and decisions and the changing economic, institutional, and cultural environment in which businessmen and firms operated from the eighteeth century to the present."

Business-government relationships had been taught for many years at the Harvard Business School. Thus, the issue was not that the School did not recognize either the topic or its importance. The real issue was one of successful implementation and critical mass. First, many of the earlier electives were idiosyncratic. They were developed and taught by great men. But the content of each course was so closely interwoven with the personality of its creator that it was difficult to transfer the teaching assignment to others. Success of the course was highly instructor-dependent. When these great professors could no longer teach their courses, it became difficult if not impossible to continue offering them. Second, the members of the BGS area were strong individualists, and it was difficult to develop a common theme or focus for the area.

Against this background Dean Fouraker in late 1972 made a bold and risky move. Instead of entrusting the expansion of the School's efforts in business-government relations to the established BGS area, he decided to abolish the area itself. He then merged its activities with those in the Business Policy (BP) area to form a new area called General Management. In the School's educational setting it was a major organizational change. Not surprisingly, it was not unanimously approved. Criticism focused on the fact that General Management was the only area in the School with two required courses: EAM and BP. Others spoke of a simple takeover of BGS by BP. It was also argued that the total size and scope of the new area was too large to be effectively administered. Interestingly, the same thought resurfaces in the Bok report: "In General Management, fresh thought may be needed to determine whether a single area can encompass so many of the disparate tasks that have devolved upon corporate headquarters during the past generation."[5]

Yet the strategy of merging BGS and BP had been carefully devised. While more controversial, it was potentially more far-reaching, promising, and rewarding than maintaining two separate areas. Two issues must be discussed here. One, what was the long-term strategy of the combined area? Two, what contribution could the old BP area make to the issues of business-government relations?

5. Page 20.

With respect to strategy, extensive discussion took place, primarily between Dean Fouraker; Associate Dean John McArthur, at that time in charge of the MBA Program; and myself as the newly appointed area chairman of what was to become General Management. We made several decisions on strategy. First, given the magnitude of the task and the limited resources, it was decided to limit the formulation and the implementation of the new strategy initially to the MBA Program; we deliberately decided to leave the executive programs, the Doctoral Program, and major project research for later.

Second, the ultimate goal would be to effectively interrelate public policy and business policy. The course in *Business Policy* was already in place. What we needed was an effective course in public policy, and it was decided to use the EAM franchise for this purpose. Thus, priority one was to restructure EAM and make it into a strong, useful, and successful course. With the business and public policy courses on equal footing, and only then, would we be ready to coordinate the two courses.

Third, by late 1972 the U.S. dollar had been devalued and the United States had ceased to be the lone superstate that could ignore international considerations in formulating its domestic economic policies. (As recently as March 1979 the Joint Economic Committee stated: "The Committee has consistently opposed diversion of monetary policy from domestic goals to secure international objectives other than in truly exceptional circumstances, and we reaffirm that position now. Monetary policy should be based primarily on the needs of the domestic economy."[6] This virtually exclusive

6. U.S. Congress, Joint Economic Committee, *The 1979 Joint Economic Report,* report on the January 1979 Economic Report of the President together with Supplementary and Additional Views, March 15, 1979 (Washington, Government Printing Office, 1979), pp. 91–92.

domestic focus is a common U.S. phenomenon. It permeates both schools of business and government as well as all walks of life. Yet it runs counter to the economic and political realities. Back in 1972, it was clear that MBAs should no longer graduate without a solid international grounding. Thus, the public-business policy interface would have to be explored and taught not only in the domestic but also in the international setting. This focus was consistent with the School's overall strategy which, under Dean Fouraker's leadership, was aimed at a broader international focus—as evidenced by the establishment of the Senior Managers Program in Europe during the fall of 1973.

Fourth, the bulk of the new General Management area's teaching assignments fell in the two required courses. For reasons of faculty development and renewal as well as to encourage greater innovation, it was decided to develop additional second-year courses. Also, elective courses would permit more specialization and greater depth than could be achieved in required courses which have to survey an entire field. The second-year elective effort was started early for courses related to BP. The already existing *Management of International Business* course was given a major charter of course development, which had been lagging in prior years, and would be more closely related to the BP course. Frederick T. Knickerbocker and M.Y. Yoshino undertook this effort. To deal in greater depth with the strategic and organizational issues of *Managing Diversification,* Malcolm S. Salter developed a course under that name based on an already existing seminar previously created by Norman A. Berg. A third elective was developed later by Michael E. Porter on *Industry and Competitive Analysis.* "The primary objective of the [ICA] course is to present explicit conceptual tools for industry and competitive analysis, and to relate them to the strategic problems of the individual company."

This course bridges *Business Policy* and *Industrial Organization*. For the electives related to EAM, however, it was decided to delay implementation until the required course had been placed on a firmer footing.

Fifth, it was decided—consistent with the School's overall strategy—to apply the general management point of view to the topic of business-government relations. We would deal with the total situation even though this brings with it greater complexity and makes issues less amenable to rigorous quantitative analysis. The point of view taken would be that of the practitioner: the focus would be on real situations with specific alternatives and final decisions to be made rather than on hypothetical models or ideal situations. Issues would be considered not only as intellectual challenges but also from an administrative point of view. The intellectual parameters of a problem have to be related to the institutional setting and to the organizational realities if meaningful analysis is to result.

It is particularly, but not exclusively, on this last dimension that the new General Management area could draw on the heritage of the former BP area. BP had lived through some of the challenges confronting the new effort in business-government. BP's focus had been integrative, its analysis multidimensional, its point of view that of the practitioner, and its issues those confronting top management. It was felt that a similar approach to the business-government phenomenon would be most promising.

The leadership position of Harvard in Business Policy was evidenced by some major reports on business education published during the late 1950s. These reports stressed the essential nature of a capstone course in business curricula. Thus, a transfer of Harvard's distinctive competence to the new field seemed a natural extension of its unique skills.

Furthermore, in earlier years *Business Policy* had been

plagued by the same problems that hindered a successful implementation of the business-government courses. The open-ended nature of the topic made the *Business Policy* course difficult to teach. As a result, the success of the course became highly instructor-dependent. Only the "great old men" seemed to be able to survive.

The multidimensionality of Business Policy easily led to superficiality of treatment, as numerous aspects were discussed only briefly. The fuzziness of top management's perennial challenges was not amenable to rigorous quantitative analysis and definitive solutions. So students often walked away more confused than enlightened.

Under the leadership of Professors Kenneth R. Andrews and C. Roland Christensen, the *Business Policy* course had been restructured so that by the early sixties it had acquired a sound conceptual framework. This framework now permitted junior faculty to survive in the classroom, it allowed meaningful and substantive case analysis by the students, and it proved highly practical and successful to graduates. Yet it encompassed the multidimensionality of the issues, the dynamic nature of the external environment and the internal resources, the personal values of the decision makers, and their social responsibility toward society. It was a methodology to deal with complexity. It accommodated open-endedness and fuzziness. It did not simplify reality to accommodate available theory. Instead, it tolerated ambiguity, it accepted constraints, limitations, and frustrations imposed by reality. The approach taken by the BP course had been further refined by some of the leading management consulting firms, heavily staffed with MBA graduates. The field of business policy or strategic planning had become a leading force both in the classroom and in business practice.

During the 1972–1973 transition we deliberately decided to attempt to transfer the BP experience to EAM. While we decided to transfer some of the BP approach to EAM, we also imposed the restriction that EAM could not solve its problems simply by incorporating existing BP materials. Rather, it had to develop its own materials and retain its public policy focus. Within five years, it was evident that the attempt had succeeded. While many contributed to this success, particularly George C. Lodge, the major tribute goes to Bruce R. Scott and John W. Rosenblum. Scott had worked closely with Christensen on the restructuring of BP. During the mid-sixties, together with John McArthur, he had conducted a major field research project on "French National Planning." According to Scott:

> One of the distinctive aspects of the [EAM] course is the use of concept of national economic strategy to view what a government is doing to influence or "manage" its economy. That concept was borrowed from *Business Policy,* and we used it first as a way to understand what the French Government was up to. Subsequently, it became clear that it was a useful way to understand government actions in many countries. The United States is probably the least comfortable fit of any country we study—in large measure because the notion of government promotion of economic growth or performance is less accepted here than elsewhere.

The revamped EAM course stands as a highly innovative course development effort that requires further discussion. Recently its name was changed to *Business, Government and the International Economy* (BGIE). In spite of recent questioning of the case method, BGIE is yet another example of its power as an educational tool. While BGIE covers a great deal of economics, its overall content is much broader. Thus, students with a strong economics background find the course fascinating. Rather than repeating what they learned in college, the course places previously acquired knowledge in a new and frequently more useful perspective. From passive absorption of theory, they move to its active application. In the multidimensional settings, they recognize both the strengths and the shortcomings of the economic theory which they brought with them. About two-thirds of our students, however, have little background in economics. (In the School's executive programs, this percentage is even higher.) For these students, the course gives them the basic and essential economic tools. The relevance and the understanding of the economic theory are enhanced by the course's situational analysis.

A partial overview of the course at this point is essential to give the reader a feel for its approach and substance. Since business school students are most familiar with company-situation cases, we begin with a transition case involving the establishment by a French company of a new tire plant in Nova Scotia in Canada to supply the U.S. market. At first glance, particularly from a production viewpoint, the decision appears absurd. Tires are bulky products, their transportation involves mostly shipping by air, and one would expect a plant to be located close to market. Also, why manufacture in Canada if 85 percent of the plant's output is destined for the U.S. market? In this instance, financial incentives provided by the provincial and federal Canadian governments have changed the economic logic. Why is Canada doing this? What is its impact on the existing Canadian tire companies, mostly subsidiaries of U.S. tire companies? What are the competitive implications for the U.S. parents since most of the new plant's output is to be exported to the United States? Are their efforts to request countervailing duties wise? This case makes clear (1) that in today's world competitive interrelationships occur among multinational companies (while previously they took place largely between domestic firms), and (2) that international competitive relationships are influenced by the relationship between each company and its government. Also, students see that government policies are frequently influenced by the competitive and cooperative relationships between countries. Thus, we have the following framework:

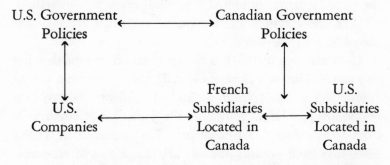

At that point, we tell the students that 90 percent of their education focuses at the bottom half of the framework. Yet the horizontal interfaces at the bottom are influenced by both the vertical interfaces and the horizontal interfaces at the top. BGIE as the only course dealing with the top of the framework will focus almost exclusively on this dimension.

After this introductory case, it is logical to discuss Canada in more detail. This leads to a better understanding of why Canada provided the financial incentives. What has been Canada's policy with respect to foreign direct investment, and why is it changing? What role has foreign equity played in the country's economic development, both in terms of benefits and costs? How much discretion does Canada have in formulating its economic policy with a huge, powerful neighbor ten times its size to the south and with other markets separated by large oceans? A critical element in understanding Canada's options and dilemmas is its balance of payments. Thus, students gain hands-on experience with this tool, and a special class is set aside to ensure that the required technical knowledge is fully understood.

Balance of payments leads to the international adjustment mechanism. International competitiveness is not only a function of a company's domestic cost and price structure but also of its country's exchange rate. What influences the level of this exchange rate? Here BGIE discusses the Gold Standard, the Gold Exchange Standard, and the Bretton Woods system. (The current system of fluctuating exchange rates is discussed later in the course.)

The fifth class in BGIE is the first session of nine devoted to Japan's economic development. It covers the time period from 1853 to 1881, quite a shock to students used to contemporary problems. Why does the Japan series begin with Commodore Perry's entrance into Tokyo harbor in 1853? First, because it permits one to trace the origins of economic development strategies, of a country's ideology and its institutions, all of which are essential to understanding the current situation. Second, the Japan case describes how an increasingly centralized government seeks to influence and control its economy, what policies and institutions it puts into place, which sectors benefit and which ones suffer. Even though the actions taken by the Japanese government during this early period are rudimentary by today's standards, they give the students an easily understood introduction to the business-government interplay. Third, the case ends with Japan suffering from a quite current problem: stagflation. The remedy provided by Finance Minister Matsukata, however, seems less tolerable by today's standards—namely, a massive dose of deflation. What impact does this have on a country's domestic economy as well as its international transactions?

The next three classes on Japan are interwoven with an introduction to national income analysis. The major attention is given to the time period stretching from the mid-twenties to the mid-thirties, which involves some dramatic reversals in Japan's economic strategies. Students are also introduced to the Great Depression as Finance Minister Takahashi sets out to introduce classic Keynesian economic policies in a pre-Keynes era. Japan is the first nation where students engage in comprehensive "country analysis" (aided by a background note authored by John Rosenblum). This analysis focuses not only on the economic parameters and options but also on the institutional and ideological background.

From Japan the course turns to the United States with a class on Herbert Hoover confronting the 1929 crash and one on the situation facing FDR in 1933. The next session deals with a significant institutional change in the mid-thirties: the Wagner Act. Its impact is illustrated by the GM-UAW conflict of 1936–1937. A fourth case on the United States describes the evolution of the Employment Act of 1946. This four-class module not only explores the economic issues confronting the United States but also provides many insights into the U.S. economic system, its changing international framework, and its underlying ideology. As these cases unfold, students recognize how the economic system, institutions, and ideology changed during the thirties and forties, leaving us with a situation that is both complex and contradictory. Understanding the relevant elements and their evolution is enhanced through the contrast with Japan which based its economic strategies on a different economic system and on different institutions and ideologies.

It is to Japan that the course returns. One session is devoted to the Occupation period and two sessions to the Japanese "economic miracle." The Japanese economic strategy, its business policies, and its institutional setting which led to its extraordinary postwar economic performance become the cornerstone of the course, and the strategies of other countries, such as the United States, Germany, France, and Britain, are contrasted with it. Japan's success further-more can be understood only in an international context, with particular emphasis on its relationship with the United States.

Thus, as BGIE turns to the economic situation confronting Richard Nixon in 1969, students are able to analyze it not only in domestic but also in international terms. We are now in class sixteen and discuss the deflationary policies under-taken to combat the 4 percent inflation resulting from an overheated economy that is unable to simultaneously digest a Great Society and the Vietnam war. Special attention is given to monetary policy, introducing students to its basic elements, its expected impact, and the resulting implications for the banking system and its borrowers. New institutional developments such as bank-holding companies and particu-larly the Eurocurrency markets as well as the demise of Penn Central in 1970 are closely related to the impact of the restrictive monetary policies.

Two years later (1971), the results of the deflationary policies are reviewed. In spite of higher unemployment, lower capacity utilization, higher interest rates, and tighter budgetary policies, inflation has actually increased. Thus, analysis shifts from "demand-pull" to "cost-push" inflation; it explores the reasons for the latter and the options avail-able to Nixon. As part of the total analysis, the international dimension begins to loom larger. The U.S. balance of pay-ments has become a major cause of concern reflecting major structural changes in the country's international competitive position as described by excerpts from the Peterson[7] report on *The United States in the Changing World Economy.*

7. Peter G. Peterson, *The United States in the Changing World Economy* (Washington, Government Printing Office, 1971). Mr. Peter-son was at that time Assistant to the President for International Eco-nomic Affairs.

This leads to an analysis of Nixon's New Economic Game Plan of August 1971 with its wage-price controls and its ultimate devaluation of the U.S. dollar. Recognizing the new role of the United States in the international economy as well as the inflation phenomenon in an excess-capacity economy is essential to understanding subsequent events. Thus, the 1971 events are explored in great detail and constantly referred to in subsequent classes.

We have now described over twenty of BGIE's fifty-four sessions, and the reader will have obtained some feel for the course's approach and substance. Country analysis continues by focusing on national development strategies in the context of the European Common Market which restricts its members' options on trade policy by abolishing internal trade controls and also seeks to influence other economic policies of member countries through coordination, such as the recent European Monetary Agreement. Cases deal with Germany, France, and the United Kingdom. The French cases permit analysis of a very sophisticated national planning system and its role in the country's economic performance. The U.K. cases include the country's relationship with the International Monetary Fund and the resulting impact of an international agency on the formulation of national economic policy. Country analysis is also applied to the development strategies of several emerging nations, such as Brazil, Mexico, Iran, Egypt, and Sri Lanka. As the course progresses, issues become more current with particular emphasis on the changing economic and political environment of the 1970s and the new economic problem of stagflation.

Having covered the approach of country analysis at great depth for both the United States and Japan and having analyzed a number of additional countries, the course turns explicitly toward the interplay of country strategies. This is done around three critical commodities: oil, food, and money.

For oil and food, producers and consumers interact and for money, lenders and borrowers interact. The international system for each of them relies heavily on private enterprise not only to manage the logistics but also to make some critical decisions in managing either surplus or scarcity. Thus, not only the interrelationship between country strategies can be explored but also that between public and business policies (the vertical interface in the earlier chart). This is the area where, for the future, integration between the BGIE and BP courses appears most promising. One such effort, in this instance between the *Production and Operations Management* and BGIE courses, has already been launched, where both courses discuss a case on Zenith, the former focusing on Zenith's manufacturing strategy and the latter on the company's attempts to reverse U.S. trade policy.

Several aspects of BGIE stand out. First, it is a truly international course that familiarizes the students with the increasingly interconnected world in which they live. Second, it relies heavily on comparative analysis which is indeed a powerful educational tool. Issues, options, and policies stand out in much sharper focus when the experiences of different countries are compared. Third, BGIE places heavy emphasis on history, which clearly is an exception for most business school courses. Fourth, while the course conveys a great deal of theory and many analytical tools, they are both rooted in situational analysis. Thus, students recognize not only the relevance but also the limitations of these theories and techniques. Fifth, the point of view of the course is not that of a business decision maker but that of a government official. In adopting this viewpoint, BGIE does not abandon the School's traditional "administrative point of view," but the administrator here is the government of a nation-state, which increasingly "manages" the business environment. To anticipate and influence government policies, managers must be able to view issues and options from that perspective as well as from their own. Sixth, BGIE recognizes the need to spend a significant amount of class time on certain countries and industries and therefore schedules an unusually large number of multiple classes on the same topic. Depth takes precedence over variety. Seventh, BGIE looks at the total situation with its multiple elements and is integrative in focus. Country analysis is not confined to the economic variables, but encompasses politics, institutions, competitive interplay, as well as ideology.

The early years of BGIE in its new form and concept were exceptionally difficult. Most of the course materials were new, and so were most of its faculty. We were concerned about student resistance to the multiclass cases and the course focus on the government point of view. As John Rosenblum said: "The challenge was to turn a concept into a course in real time. We learned as we went." Initially, the course attempted to cover not only its current content but also the regulatory aspects of the business-government interface. In year three of the redesigned course we decided that it was impossible to cover both topics in depth and that we should eliminate the regulatory portion from the course.

BGIE today is ready for the next phase of its development. Now that for 1979–1980 the first half of the *Business Policy* course has been moved into the first year,[8] it is hoped that the integrative approach between public and business policy through joint or interrelated cases can be pushed forward. Greater emphasis will also be given to field cases and to the process through which public policies are formulated. The latter type case would also permit a bridging between public

8. Even though this move was proposed several years earlier, it took until the spring of 1979 for the faculty to vote this change. Faculty meetings often move at the same slow speed as the Congress and for similar reasons!

and business policies as the role of organizations such as the Business Roundtable are taken into account.

By 1976 BGIE was deemed to be in sufficiently strong shape to embark on the next phase of the planned area strategy: the introduction of new second-year electives. At a two-day planning meeting the area faculty explored a number of options and settled on the following program: First, since BGIE by deliberately concentrating on country analysis had been forced to abandon issues of government regulation which had been part of its initial charter, it was decided to revive this important aspect of business-government relations through a second-year elective to be called *Managing in a Regulated Environment* (MRE). Second, since BGIE's focus was largely on the industrialized world, it was felt that additional attention should be given to the developing world, where substantial economic and business opportunities lie ahead. Thus, a totally new course on *Management in Developing Countries* (MDC) was started. Third, it was decided to delete temporarily the old course on *The Business Administrator and Government Policy* (Bagpipes) in order to review its role within the overall curriculum and to devote major new course development to it. Fourth, two senior faculty members were interested in offering second-year seminars, which could potentially be enlarged to full courses, around topics on which they had accumulated a great deal of expertise in other settings. George Lodge had developed a highly successful elective in the Advanced Management Program on *Business and Ideology* and decided to transfer this course development effort to the MBA Program as a seminar entitled *Managerial Implications of Ideological Change.* Louis T. Wells, Jr., had spent several years doing research on concession agreements for various raw materials, and he was interested in broadening this knowledge to explore the important interrelationship between *Multinational*

Business and National Governments. Parallel to these developments in the General Management area a second-year course was launched by John R. Meyer and Robert A. Leone in the Production and Operations Management area, also focusing on the impact of regulation: *Government Regulation and Operating Policy.*

In planning second-year electives, the area was guided by a simple framework:

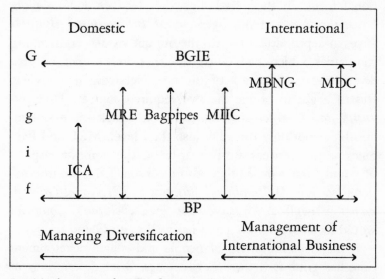

In this framework "G" denotes the government at the level of the nation-state. Its impact on the business environment is through broad economic activities, such as monetary, fiscal, and trade policies, or wage and price controls. In contrast to big G, little "g" refers to the maze of government agencies that regulate business activities. Whereas G usually affects all business, g frequently impacts only certain industries. At the bottom of the chart, "f" refers to the firm. This is the bread-and-butter focus of the School that deals primarily with company decisions. Above f, we have "i" for industry. In many foreign countries the major strategic decisions are made not at the company but at the industry level. But even in the United States, regulatory and other forces increasingly require a focus on the industry.

Such a rough framework obviously can only be a broad guide, and most courses will only imperfectly fit a given category. Nevertheless, it appeared that the two required courses covered the top and the bottom level, respectively, with both encompassing a domestic as well as an international focus. In Business Policy, the electives on *Managing Diversification* and *Management of International Business* gave in-depth attention to the unique issues confronting companies which had engaged either in product or area diversification. The task of the new electives, in our view, was to begin to bridge the two required courses. Thus, *Industry and Competitive Analysis* would look more systematically at not only the f but also the i level. MRE and Bagpipes would concentrate primarily on the domestic aspects of g and i but would relate also to G and f. In the international setting, *Multinational Business and National Governments* as well as *Management in Developing Countries* would focus heavily on g and i as well as on G and f.

A major commitment of people and course development time has gone into these new courses. Brief descriptions of each of them may be in order.

The *Managing in the Regulated Environment* course was developed jointly by Tom McCraw and Dan Kasper, and was taught during the fall of 1977 by McCraw and the following year by Kasper. The course familiarizes students with the institutional and legal arrangements that shape the business environment, particularly with respect to competition. MRE develops an appreciation of the strategic significance of regulation for the firm as well as a range of practitioner strategies open to managers facing particular regulatory situations. It focuses also on anticipating the likely shape and impact of future public policies. To provide depth, the course gives intensive attention to four industries: public utilities, air transport, telecommunications, and automobiles. It devotes some time, however, to cross-industry social and environmental regulation by such agencies as OSHA and EPA. The course takes an "inside-outside" approach by frequently including at least two viewpoints, one public and one private. For example, in the airline regulation cases, the class analyzes issues from the perspectives of the Civil Aeronautics Board, the CEO of a trunkline carrier, and the CEO of an airframe manufacturer. A second aspect of the "inside-outside" approach is reflected in the course materials.

> Here the practical and managerial aspects of the topics, represented by the cases, will be balanced against the theoretical and institutional aspects, represented by carefully chosen selections from the immense body of scholarly literature on regulation. The inherently multi-disciplinary nature of the subject will emerge from the legal, economic, political, and historical sources used as background materials.

Management in Developing Countries became largely the responsibility of James E. Austin. The course resulted from a concern that the School's curriculum did not adequately deal with the problems and managerial environment in the developing countries. Given their growing socioeconomic and demographic importance, Jim Austin describes his experience as follows:

> The first challenge was how to distill a broad field like management in developing countries into a manageable scope with a meaningful focus. . . . My original objective stressed (a) developing an understanding of the economic development process, (b) the public management of that process, and (c) the management of private firms within the LDC environment. This was overly ambitious. A closer scrutiny of the international business and economic development litera-

ture led me to conclude that a real conceptual gap in the field was the absence of a systematic framework for analyzing the distinctive characteristics of the developing country environments and understanding their managerial implications. Consequently, I narrowed my objectives to developing such a framework. Familiarity with this framework would strengthen the student's managerial capacity to operate effectively in the LDC environment. This narrowing of the objectives was accompanied by a sharper focus on certain dimensions of the LDC environment. The MDC course is based on the premise that there are certain distinctive characteristics about the developing country environments and these carry special managerial implications. The special nature of the LDC environment emerges because of its different level and process of development compared to the more industrialized nations. . . . I have chosen three salient and interrelated characteristics which I believe are particularly relevant to management and appear to be present in most developing countries:

- *High Government Involvement*—consequently, a critical aspect of operating in an LDC is the management of the business-government relationship; to understand the differences in public and private perspectives, social cost benefit analysis concepts and techniques are presented; furthermore, some cases are presented from the public manager's perspective, others from the private, and still others from both;

- *Low Productivity*—this leads us to focus on issues of technology utilization; here we draw on technology transfer, choice, and adaptation concepts;

- *Market Imperfections*—the functioning of free market mechanisms is generally impeded by factors such as infrastructural deficiencies, concentration and imbalance of economic resources; thus, we focus on the analysis of market structures.

The examination of these areas draws on concepts from the economic development and international business literature. Having narrowed the scope, I then faced two additional challenges: how to extend the BGIE concepts and how to analyze external dependencies.

· *Extending the BGIE Concepts*—The second challenge became how to link the "country analysis" skills developed by BGIE (EAM) to the managerial tasks of formulating corporate strategy. A standard BGIE country analysis examines the national political and economic strategies, performance and context at the macro-level. The issue is what meaning do those have for a business manager. A conceptual mechanism which I use for relating macro-level government strategies to micro-level decision making is what I term *Policy Instrumentation Analysis*. BGIE "national strategies" only have relevance to a firm to the extent that they affect the firm's operations. This effect flows from the specific policy instruments which governments use to implement their strategy. Thus, national strategies get translated into macro policies (e.g., monetary, fiscal, trade, agriculture) which are implemented through various types of policy instruments (e.g., administrative, legal, executive) which in turn can impact negatively or positively on various aspects of corporate strategy (e.g., finance, production, procurement, marketing, organization, competition). With this framework, students can *selectively* analyze macro policies and *systematically* examine the corresponding policy instruments to ascertain implications for corporate strategy. Thus, this MDC framework is an attempt at fusing BGIE and BP skills and concepts within a particular environmental setting.

· *Analyzing External Dependencies*—A firm's environment obviously consists of more than just government policies. There are many economic, political, social, and ideologi-

cal forces which surround the firm. Thus, a third challenge was how to relate these external factors to corporate strategy. Generally, these forces manifest themselves
through the actions of other institutions which interact
with the firm either as factor suppliers, consumers, competitors, coordinators or regulators. Thus, our environmental analysis framework must also analyze the nature
of these external dependencies and their implications
for corporate strategy. A useful conceptual tool for dealing with these dimensions is *systems analysis*. Although
I have applied this component of the framework in the
course, it is still in a stage of development. I am exploring the possible fusion of concepts from systems theory
(e.g., Churchman, Berlinski), organizational behavior
(e.g., Levine and White, Benson, Mendlin and Aldrich,
Kotter), industrial organization (Porter, Caves), and
agribusiness (Goldberg). This process involves the development of a framework and analytical mode for
identifying crucial interrelationships and analyzing in a
penetrating way their strategic implications.

Lou Wells developed *Multinational Business and National Governments,* which has now become a full course. It
deals with the different views that private foreign investors
and governments hold about the benefits and costs of projects. It then explores the problems and solutions managers
have found when they try to reach investment agreements
with governments on matters such as taxation and ownership. Topics covered are various forms of agreements (joint
ventures, production sharing, etc.) and different financial
arrangements as well as the tools used by different types of
countries: state enterprises in Western Europe, MITI in
Japan, co-production arrangements in Eastern Europe. The
course subsequently treats problems that foreign firms encounter during the life of their projects. What are the on-
going problems of government relations with home and host

governments? What kinds of lobbying efforts are appropriate and effective for various kinds of problems? As this point, bribery and extortion in international business is discussed. Since many foreign investors eventually face government pressures for change, the course deals with renegotiations, programmed changes in ownership (such as those acquired by the Andean Group), and nationalizations and expropriations. The course also contrasts the various approaches and policy instruments governments use to control foreign investors. Finally, a few classes are devoted to the problems managers face in negotiating with several governments simultaneously and the activities of international organizations that are concerned with the actions of multinational firms.

The Business Administrator and Government Policy course has been restructured for 1979–1980 by J. Ronald Fox. He has incorporated into this course certain segments from George Lodge's seminar on *Managerial Implications of Ideological Change,* which in turn has now been deleted temporarily. The course is described as being concerned with

the development and implementation of effective strategies employed by corporations in managing their business-government relations. It establishes the need for such strategies by examining the problems posed by changing external forces and increasing involvement of diverse government agencies in matters affecting large business corporations.

· · · · ·

Section I examines the developments occurring in society which lead to increasing involvement of government in business activities. This section explores the changing rights and duties of individuals, corporations, and branches of government in dealing with current social and economic problems. Students will examine the changing roles of (1) marketplace competition, (2) government controls, and (3) business-government participation as mechanisms for governing the activities of corporations in society.

. . . . .

As a result of the expanding involvement of government in business activities, it becomes increasingly important for business managers to understand the government decision-making process. As such, Section II includes an analysis of this process in terms of its institutions, participants, and the characteristic subsystems through which it operates. The types of materials to be used in this section will include cases and notes to illustrate a conceptual model of the government decision-making process as a series of interrelated subsystems, each with a few participants from the legislative branch, executive branch, state governments, business, and other special interest groups.

. . . . .

Section III explores the manner in which business managers are involved with various parts of the Federal Government. This section includes:

1. An examination of the various mechanisms employed by business managers to participate in the development and implementation of government policies and programs. This section includes an examination of the roles of institutions such as the corporate office of government affairs, the Business Roundtable, and business and trade associations.

2. An examination of the activities of business managers as they develop and implement effective strategies and tactics for dealing with the government. This section develops and explores models for conflict resolution of business-government issues. These include activities in which business managers serve as integrators of diverse public interest goals and as catalysts for trade-off decisions among the various objectives of business internal departments, government agencies, and special interest groups.

Looking back at six years of course development activities in the new General Management area, we can be proud of what has been accomplished. Yet much remains to be done. When we started the new area, the *Business Policy* course was in good shape. With so much to be done we diverted resources from the course and had to give low priority to its further development. With the new courses now in place, the time has come aggressively to move the BP course forward again. The BP course can now consider innovative approaches that were hitherto impossible, because by moving it partially into the first year BP and BGIE can begin to explore jointly the interface between public and business policies.

The new developments created over the last six years can also be transferred to the School's executive programs. Some of this has already occurred as BGIE materials have been introduced in both the Program for Management Development and the Advanced Management Program. Beyond the transfer of MBA materials, the executive programs are a natural place for integrative course development, and work has started on this dimension.

Also, the time has come to pursue more research. With the large number of teaching requirements, the area was and continues to be stretched. Also, until a more focused approach to the vast topic of business-government relations was developed, research, particularly by junior faculty, would have been risky. But now the time appears ripe, and new efforts are underway. Tom McCraw is working on a book on regulation. Bruce Scott has embarked on a comparative project exploring economic performance. George Lodge is continuing to develop the concept of ideology as an integrated way of understanding the choices confronting government and business policy makers in the United States and other countries. Gale Merseth has just completed his thesis on "Regulation and Income Redistribution: The Massachusetts Experience."

In any academic endeavor the crucial variable in the final analysis is people. Thus, this discussion will end on this dimension. During the six years of the new General Management area, thirteen new faculty were hired and five were brought in from other School activities. Of the eighteen, six have left. The remaining twelve faculty plus four colleagues who previously belonged to the BGS area make up the sixteen area members who are primarily interested in and working on the business-government interface. Of the sixteen, seven have tenure, four hold an associate and four an assistant professorship, while one is a special lecturer.

The range of backgrounds and expertise is broad: four faculty members come from business history, two have legal training, two come from international business, two from business policy, one from political science, one from economics, two from journalism, one from business with expertise in military procurement, and one is a BGIE doctoral graduate. Four of the sixteen have government experience at both the state and federal level, some of it in high positions. The approach of the group is multidisciplinary in a true sense. Different viewpoints and approaches are common as faculty members continue to explore the difficult challenge of the business-government interface.

The conclusion of this paper should address two issues. One, what lessons appropriate for the emerging University-wide program in Business and Public Policy can we draw from the recent Business School experience? Two, which topics in the enormously vast field of business-government relations deserve major strategic attention to avoid the danger of Harvard's spreading its resources too thin?

One important aspect relates to the multidimensional courses to be taught: without a conceptual framework they are likely to encounter trouble and become a graveyard for younger (and often older) faculty. With a conceptual framework, as has happened in BP and BGIE, both course and faculty development are possible. *Second,* given the enormous scope of the business-government field, a team effort is essential. Given the highly individualistic orientation of most university professors, this does not come easily and places a premium on the proper organization and leadership of the planned activities. *Third,* a generalist orientation and different disciplinary backgrounds will be equally important. In a university milieu which rewards specialization, such people face an uphill climb. *Fourth,* the faculty needed to address the business-government issues can rarely be hired from other places; it will involve a major task of internal faculty development. *Fifth,* the pedagogical approach of looking at issues from different points of view, such as the "inside-outside" approach in MRE or the government focus in BGIE, has proved very successful. It promises an even greater payoff through the planned Government-Business School interface. *Sixth,* when confronted with the dilemma of whether to cover a large number of topics in the business-government field versus concentrating in depth on a limited number, the latter approach has proved more successful. *Seventh,* both a historical and international focus, permitting a comparative approach, greatly enhances the pedagogical effectiveness of the courses. *Finally,* the point needs to be repeated that the great challenge of the business-government interface lies as much in the administrative implementation of a strategy as it does in the intellectual formulation of that strategy. Abstract theories will not by themselves improve the state of the art. This can be done only through effective teaching, innovative course development which is rooted in real-life situations, and integrative research which has meaning for academicians and practitioners alike.

Which topics deserve strategic attention is an issue which ought to be addressed early in the life of the new University-wide program. From the vantage point of the Business School, the simple framework used in focusing the General Management activities may be useful. One level of integration may focus on the big G: the government policies influencing the state of the economy. With productivity increasingly becoming the key to enhancing economic growth, reducing inflation, and stabilizing the exchange rate, the business-government relationship during the eighties will have to take a form very different from that of prior decades. Continuing the existing policies and approaches will almost surely lead to economic stagnation with its inevitable social tensions. The alternate, and in my view feasible, approach to economic prosperity will require two major shifts in orientation: from demand to supply management and from an emphasis on consumption to stress on investment. The government and business policies required to get us there constitute a largely new agenda. The new University-wide program ought to be in the forefront of this new challenge.

Another line of inquiry may focus on the "i" or industry level of the framework. The current interface between government and business takes place largely between economic policies and regulatory activities on one side and single business firms on the other. Yet many of the issues impact entire industries. In the decade ahead, will business and government be able to work together in formulating cohesive strategies for some of the country's major industries? There are many hurdles. Most of our monetary and fiscal policies deal with the economy in aggregates, not with specific industries. The antitrust laws are a formidable obstacle. Also, companies perceive their opportunities differently and pursue separate strategies. But equally if not more powerful forces may lead us to more of an industry-wide approach. For example, can the country afford to let its steel industry slowly slide down-hill while caught between inadequate cash flow, low stock market values, limited debt capacity, strong import competi-tion, heavy environmental burdens, limited capacity, old plants, and price-sensitive buyers? This example could easily be expanded and applied equally to many other industries. The agenda here, too, is a new one. If the country is viewed as consisting structurally of many different industries, is there not a similarity with the diversified corporation? If yes, to what extent are some of the strategic planning ap-proaches which have been introduced in diversified corpora-tions during the last fifteen years applicable to national policy? What role, if any, is national planning to play? This topic again seems a logical candidate for the new University-wide program.

This conclusion has ignored the obvious need for business and government to become more familiar with the problems and perspectives of the other. Obviously, EPA, OSHA, SEC, ERISA, affirmative action, consumer protection, and a host of other regulatory activities will continue to be important during the next decade. This topic obviously needs more analysis and understanding and clearly has to be included in the joint effort. It may well be, however, that in large firms in industries heavily affected by the public interest the growth phase of regulation is over and new forms of busi-ness-government cooperation or partnership are emerging. It is to be hoped that the new program of cooperation be-tween the School of Government and the Business School will give attention not only to yesterday's developments but also to the new agenda of issues in business-government relations that will mark the coming decade.

7 | Business and Public Policy

JOHN T. DUNLOP

Lamont University Professor
Harvard University

The Central Concerns

THE LAST DECADE has seen a vast expansion in the scope and detail of government regulation of business decisions, beyond those of the New Deal era, beyond public utility industries, and beyond temporary periods of wage and price controls. It is ironical, and yet indicative of the basic character of these developments, that a flood of new legislation emerged in eight years of Republican Administration. The cluster of regulations growing around environmental protection, health and safety, pension plans, energy development and utilization, and consumer protection are all illustrative of a qualitatively different business environment. Older agencies also have penetrated much further into internal business decisions, as in the case of disclosure rules of the Securities and Exchange Commission, the Federal Trade Commission's quest for data, and the emergence of goals and time tables in affirmative action programs. Even private price and wage decisions in some sectors are under continuing and systematic scrutiny.

But more pervasive rules and regulations of administrative agencies is not a sufficient measure of the extent of the opening up of private business decisions to public scrutiny and review. The courts have raised the risks of damages in many new areas, and "public interest" law groups have enhanced the range of policy litigation and have to a considerable measure become an independent means of public policy determination.

Reference should also be made to the role of Congressional committees with their enlarged staffs and to the press and the media in shaping the agenda and the climate for many business decisions.

But this new and perplexing setting for decision making of business enterprises also raises larger questions of the future relations of the business community as a whole to government and the community. The business interests in our society do not have an effective mechanism or procedure to reconcile their internal conflicting interests on a wide range of public policy issues. Business views that receive public attention often appear as extreme and reflect antisocial practices by a few enterprises or sectors. Such practices adversely reflect upon all business. While it must be recognized that our business community in its relationships to government and among enterprises is very different from those in Japan or Germany, illustrated by our antitrust laws, there are serious consequences arising from the independence and separateness of businesses and the absence of business consensus on emerging issues.

Stanley Marcus, a thoughtful business leader, has well said:

Who among the business community today would seriously propose that Congress repeal our child labor laws—or the Sherman Anti-Trust Act? The Federal Reserve Act, the Security Exchange Act? Or Workman's Compensation: Or Social Security? Or Minimum wage? Or Medicare? Or civil rights legislation? All of us today recognize that such legislation is an integral part of our system; that it has made us a stronger, more prosperous nation—and, in the long run, has been good for business. But we can take precious little credit for any of the social legislation now on the books, for business vigorously opposed most of this legislation—and we get precious little credit from the people. . . .[1]

The absence of effective leadership for the business community on many questions, in consensus building and dealing with other groups and governments, means that business enterprises forfeit almost entirely to politicians the development of common views within business itself. The rapid expansion of governmental regulations in recent years, and specifically government's penchant for rigid, bureaucratic "command and control" regulations even when ineffective or counter-productive, arises in part from a lack of coherence and consensus within the business community about more constructive alternatives for achieving social purposes.

Thus, in the individual business enterprise and in the business community as a whole there is a new and more complex setting in dealing with government and the community. The significance of these elements may be expected to grow and to put new demands on business executives and leaders.

The American community, contrary to some views, does basically respect and have confidence in the ability of business executives. In war time, large segments of mobilization of economic resources have been assigned to business executives. In the fiscal crisis of New York City, business leaders

1. "Can Free Enterprise Survive Success?" Omaha, Neb.: The University of Nebraska at Omaha, November 18, 1975.

were asked to take over major functions and to resolve tough issues that politicians had avoided or postponed to the brink of bankruptcy. In some metropolitan localities the business community has played a major role in economic development, urban renewal, and racial integration of schools. Increasingly, at local and national levels, the community is calling upon the skills and qualities of business executives in many areas of public business.

This new setting raises serious problems for government administrators and program officers, no less than for business executives. Both groups are thrown into much contact with each other, typically in a sharp adversary position, usually with legal staffs. They have different backgrounds; approach issues with different time horizons; see the press and media in quite different roles; and have quite different institutional objectives; and frequently have quite different personal values. They see the role of the law in society in substantially different ways, one to change and the other largely to preserve. The business perspective often tends to be international, while the government administrator is much more narrowly national. They are also often separated by a gap in age and experience. It is little wonder that beyond difficult substantive issues and values they do not find it easy to communicate with each other.

There is a critical need in the education of both business executives and public administrators, particularly in executive-level programs, for each to understand not merely the substantive issues of these areas of governmental activity and the decision making processes of business and government but also to appreciate the setting, constraints, and personal context in which the opposite number operates.

The present career patterns of business and government executives and administrators warrant review and adjust-

ment in personnel and compensation policies in both careers
to facilitate development of more sensitive and perceptive
business leaders and more understanding and competent
government officials. It would be helpful if more business
enterprises could plan to provide a period of time, such as
two to four years, for more executives to work in government as a normal part of their development. Similarly,
present governmental executives should be encouraged to
spend comparable periods in private industry. A greater
degree of two-way mobility across the public–private line
would in time make a major contribution to dealing with
the issues of isolation and parochialism raised earlier. This
would require that our present conflict of interest concepts,
as they are practiced, be changed significantly. Even within
the present framework of attitudes, more could be done to
enhance interchange through recruitment policies, particularly in the government.

The Business School and the Public Policy Program

The Harvard Business School has been training for business careers and decision making for many years, and its
distinguished record is well known. In 1975 there were
5,187 alumni of Harvard Business School with the title
President or Chairman of the Board, which represents about
one in eight of the school's graduates.

Since World War II a variety of executive-level programs
have been introduced. The use of cases and other materials
to focus upon hard decision making contrasts with the disciplinary emphasis of traditional graduate study at universities. In the selection of cases and problems, and in response
to the professional interests of its faculty and the view of
outside advisory groups including alumni, the Business
School has sought to reflect some of the new complex prob-

lems of relations to government sketched above. But a substantial intensification of this effort is in order, in parallel development with the Public Policy program concentrated in the School of Government, to focus on business decisions in the complex environment of new government roles and to make a contribution to business understanding and strategies in the process of public policy making.

The Harvard Public Policy Program, centered in the School of Government, is portrayed in President Bok's Report for 1973–74.[2] He stated two ambitions for Harvard's School of Government in the decade ahead. First, that the School become a substantial professional school doing for the public sector much of what Harvard's Schools of Business, Law, and Medicine do for their respective private professions; second, that the School serve as a hub around which faculty and students in all the Schools of the University are mobilized and focused on critical issues of public policy.

The School of Government attempts to provide professional education of the highest quality for positions of significant responsibility in the public sector. Through the case method, the School concentrates on decision making in the public sector and now offers three main courses of study.

The *first* is a two-year program begun in 1969 leading to the Master of Public Policy degree. Analogous to the MBA, this program is designed for recent college graduates with two or three years of public experience who are contemplating careers in public service. The entering class of MPPs now numbers 50; the five-year plans call for increasing the group to 110 a class.

The *second* course of study is a one-year midcareer course

2. *President's Report to the Board of Overseers,* Harvard University 1973–74.

of study leading to a Master's in Public Administration. Enrolling 140 students this year, this program has been a part of the School of Public Administration for many years. It provides advanced training for officials who have already achieved positions of substantial responsibility in the civil, diplomatic, and military services. It enables the established professional to reevaluate his or her past experience while acquiring new skills and competences.

The *third* group of courses is comprised of executive training programs. The fourth Program for Senior Managers in Government will be held during the summer of 1979 under joint sponsorship of the School of Government and the Business School. The program will enroll select senior managers representing federal, state, and local governments. Since government administrators have very diversified backgrounds in graduate education, the most effective way to provide professional managerial and public policy education is to press forward with the development of executive-level programs, drawing into the university government administrators and policy makers for short-term programs. Such programs are genuinely professional and require experienced faculty interested and able to teach such practitioners. Plans call for continued expansion of the executive training programs year-round to enroll 500 senior government managers annually by 1983. The students who have gone through these programs have held a wide variety of significant posts.

Through its Institute of Politics, the School also offers a number of short-term programs for newly elected mayors, governors, and members of Congress. The third class of new Congressmen, numbering 35, was in Cambridge for the week of December 12–19, 1976. Reactions to this program have been so enthusiastic that the School has accepted Congressional Reference Service support to expand the size and scope of the activity. Discussions are underway with the Conference of Governors, Conference of Mayors, and others for a similar expansion of other short courses for elected officials.

The Public Policy Programs in the School of Government are intended to pioneer in the development of materials and approaches for public sector decision makers and at the same time to be a resource and to provide modules for specialized areas of public policy in which Harvard has professional schools: education, health, law, and city and regional planning.

Commenting on the importance of the new public policy effort in the University, President Bok's *Report* concludes:

> We may well be approaching the threshold of the new era of scarcity and restraint in which the deficiences of government cannot be papered over to constantly rising levels of prosperity. Moreover, we have certainly moved beyond the era when any important group can afford to harbor the belief that ineffective government will leave them free to pursue their private interests. Like it or not, public officials will establish the framework that determines the ability of each segment of society to achieve its goals. . . . Since universities are primarily responsible for advanced training in our society, they share a unique opportunity and obligation to prepare a profession of public servants equipped to discharge these heavy responsibilities to the nation.

These convictions have led President Bok to place his highest priority and commitment, among the numerous claims for resources at Harvard University, on this Public Policy Program. Its success will require development of innovative materials and staff, establishment of close, effective interaction between the School of Government and other major Schools at Harvard, and, over time, the emergence of new personnel policies in government and other sectors. Harvard is seeking $21 million for the Public Policy Program and the School of Government.

Proposal

As a part of the University-wide program in Public Policy, the present proposal requests that capital funds be made available to provide four tenured professors, assistant professors, and supporting staff for research and case material development in the area of Business and Public Policy. Two tenured professors are to be located in the School of Government (Public Policy Program) and the other two in the Business School, to work together as a coordinated team.

The four tenured appointments are to be considered together to assure that the proposed teaching, course development, and research is fully harmonized. President Bok will appoint a joint search committee and will personally chair the *ad hoc* committee to review both appointments. To assure that the four professors, and the related junior staff and research personnel continue to be devoted to the purposes of the proposed activities, the President intends to appoint a university professor as his representative to work directly with this new program.

The plan is that the professors will work together as a team to develop cases and other materials for use in programs—particularly executive programs—in the two schools. A case, or part of a case, will look at problems of formulating legislation and regulations and handling issues from the perspective of public policy officials; a companion case, or part of a case, will consider the same problem from the perspective of business decision making and the business community. Two professors would jointly teach a course using these cases in the Business School, and a second course in the Public Policy Program. In addition, they would jointly offer an advanced course open to students from both Schools and would share other teaching assignments. The vital point is to bring full appreciation of both perspectives and of the roles of both sets of decision makers and administrators to each other.

A wide range of topics and issues would be used in a co-ordinated fashion to illustrate the need for business executives and public administrators both to become more familiar with the problems and perspectives of the other. Current issues that would be taught in this way include:

- Environmental Protection Agency regulations and automobile emissions standards
- S.E.C. disclosure rules and commission and agent practices to secure business in some overseas areas
- Clean air legislation and business location
- Energy policy issues including coal, nuclear, natural gas, and oil
- The pension regulation area and its impact
- Occupational health regulations and business policies
- Affirmative action regulations and personnel policies
- Health care regulation
- Consumer protection regulation and specific illustrative products
- Arab boycott legislation and regulations and overseas business operations
- Bilateral trade negotiations, dumping, and other aspects of government regulation in international trade developed by problems of particular products. The topic should include East–West trade, technology and trade questions, and government financing and tax issues

- Governmental personnel and compensation policies and their impact on private business
- Government policies to restrain business price increases and compensation increases

To give an example of how this parallel process works, consider the issues of occupational health and safety. Case-based classroom discussion would start by reviewing the experience with Workman's Compensation and seek to illuminate the role of political processes, interest group pressures, professional societies, the media, and the courts from which the Occupational Health and Safety Act of 1970 emerged. By examining in detail a number of specific examples like regulations affecting noise abatement, or factory equipment, or coke ovens, the cases would illustrate vividly what has now come to be recognized as a "regulatory syndrome": a new agency (OSHA) created by Congress to fix a problem attempts to proscribe a list of uniformly prescribed rules and regulations that direct all regulatees in a "command and control" fashion to take specific steps; requests for interpretation and exception on grounds of differences among regulatees are handled by a cumbersome adjudicatory process that cannot keep pace with change in the area; inspection and enforcement issues are reviewed; eventually, central policy issues are transferred to the courts by either regulatees or "public interest" groups for lengthy litigation. Study of this process should include consideration of the long-term consequences of such regulations on technological change, investment, employment, and market changes. Through careful exploration of such cases, students shall be encouraged to gain a broader appreciation of the impact of regulation on business and an understanding of alternative strategies to minimize the burdens, frictions and delays that so often characterize "command and control" regulation. The second part of this case or group of cases would pursue these issues from the perspective of private managers of a firm subject to OSHA regulations on noise or plant safety. By carefully reviewing an array of options—from seeking to influence the legislation and regulations, living with the regulations, to requesting exceptions, or fighting the regulations, or circumventing their application—students should get a clear sense of the consideration that must bear on prudent managerial policies.

Taught in the Business School, somewhat more class time might be spent on the business perspective, and in the School of Government, more on the public policy issues. But in both courses the distinctive purpose of this twin approach would be to infuse into each course a greater degree of understanding of the practical impact and consequences of the other world of decision making. In addition, students from the two Schools would meet for joint classes to provide for each an even livelier appreciation of what the problems look like from each perspective. Among the most important lessons that would emerge from careful examination of a problem like occupational health and safety regulations are the limits of government's standard regulatory approach and the necessity to explore alternatives; the importance of understanding the ways in which government regulations affect the incentives and behavior of private managers on whose action success of social objectives depend; the need for business managers to understand the political, administrative, and legal process from which regulations emerge and to involve themselves earlier in the development of regulations (and the forms of regulation) to make possible more effective achievement of both business and government objectives.

The gathering of materials and the organization of ideas was begun during the academic year 1976–77 in a faculty

seminar drawn from the Schools of Law, Business, Public
Health, and the Kennedy School on the subject of the Reform of the Regulatory Process. The seminar is now an
established part of the research program.

The range of potential cases is rich in experience and
lessons for both business executives and governmental administrators. Consider the narrow question of the role and
activities of the Washington office of a company and its
relations to various levels of officers in the company and in
governmental agencies. A comparison of the experience of
different companies would be mutually instructive. Or, consider the problems for government and business in seeking
to resolve the conflicting interest of the auto industry and
the basic metals and power industries over the Clean Air
Act amendments. Or, take the very large issues of business–
labor–government posed by the Bullock report in England
and Sudreau report in France and the question of the future
of these issues in this country.

The joint team approach will also be applied to the executive training programs of the two schools. Students from
the two groups of executive programs would be combined
in the same classes on some issues; additionally, the professors would stimulate informal contacts. In view of the
diverse group of executive and professional programs in the
University, similar systematic interactions over case materials
will be arranged with health care administrators, Nieman
fellows (from the press and media), local and regional
officials, newly elected politicians, and overseas counterparts
from government, labor, and business.

The Harvard Business School has pioneered not only in
case development but in systems to distribute those cases to
universities across the country. The School of Government
is now in the process of developing a similar national network for schools of public policy and management. There-

fore, through the intercollegiate case clearinghouse and other syndicated distribution channels, one could be assured that the work done under the auspices of these parallel professors would be shared by business and government schools throughout the nation.

The cooperation and coordination described in this proposal has been facilitated by construction of a new building for the School of Government, located diagonally across the river from the Business School. Proximity of location is a considerable advantage to faculty, students, and alumni in arranging areas of coordination.

The separate but coordinated character of the appointments is fundamental to these proposals. It is essential that two of the senior persons be regular members of the Business School faculty, and the other two be regular members of the School of Government. These separate appointments are in no way likely to diminish their cooperation and joint activities; indeed, their combined effectiveness with the academic community and outside will be significantly enhanced by the proposed arrangements. In this sense, several joint appointments might not be nearly as effective, since professors holding such appointments do not always have the influence enjoyed by full-time members of a school's faculty.

The supporting staff and resources for each senior appointment should include an assistant professor, case writers, research assistants, and related expenses. Only with these normal complements can the most effective teaching and development of cases and materials be carried forward. The program should be directed by the two professors with the assistance of the President's representative.

This complementary approach is a new concept. It will help decision makers in business to be more aware of public policy issues, and government policy makers and administrators to be more aware of business impacts. Analogous appointments are contemplated in other fields between the same pair of schools and with other professional schools. The fields of public personnel policy, health care policy, international economic policies, and public policies relating to plant and equipment (capital formation) offer fertile ground for such cooperation.

Summary

PROPOSAL

Capital funds be made available for four tenured professors, assistant professors, and supporting staff for case material development and research, in the area of Public Policy and Business, one to be located in the Business School and the other in the School of Government (Public Policy Program), to work together as a coordinated team.

CASES: MATERIALS AND CURRICULAR DEVELOPMENT

Cases will be developed that span in a wide variety of particular situations the process of public policy development and the process of business decision making. The focus will be on government and business decision making and their interaction. Illustrative of the range of substantive issues are the following:

· Environmental Protection Agency relations and automobile emissions standards
· Pension regulation
· Occupational health and safety[1]
· Clean air and business location
· Affirmative action regulation
· Health care regulation

1. For fuller discussion of one example, see page 000.

- Consumer protection regulation
- S.E.C. disclosure rules and overseas commissions and practices
- Arab boycott legislation and regulation
- Bilateral trade negotiations
- Wage and price restraints

PROGRAMS AND STUDENTS

These cases and materials will be used in both the masters and executive level programs in the Business School and the School of Government. They will provide business executives a deeper appreciation of the full range of governmental processes, and in turn provide government program officers a better appreciation of corporate decision making and of the impact of government regulation on business. At executive training levels in the Business School, these cases will provide a block of materials in the Advance Management and Middle Management programs, and in the Kennedy School they will be used in the new executive programs.

Both professors will teach in both programs. Provision will be made for a series of joint sessions and discussions so that both business executives and government program officers can discuss cases together.

These case materials will be distributed through a national network to other professional schools, both business schools, and a growing number of schools of public policy and management.

CAREERS

One of the central concerns of this program, and the four professors, will be the development of research on careers in government and the means to facilitate mobility among government, business, education, labor organizations, and other organizations in the society. The research will look toward proposals to overcome the major obstacles to such mobility at present, and it should seek to use the resources of the placement services in this University to achieve that objective.

RESEARCH

Paired professors will develop areas of substantive research and writing in the interaction of government and business decision making. Their research should span the interaction of government and business, seeking to overcome the disciplinary separation and isolation of the past.